This phrase book, in a .... e
readily understood on all everyday occasions; to get you quickly
and easily, *where* you want and *what* you want; and to enable you
to cope with those minor problems and emergencies that always
seem to arise on holiday.

A pronunciation guide accompanies each phrase, the topic of
which can quickly be found by reference to the contents list or
index. Subjects include: customs, medical treatment, shopping,
sightseeing, restaurants, cafés and bars.

ayn mahattat al-bas ?
— where is the bus-stop

ARABIC
PHRASE BOOK

A. Khouri Velarde, L. Coleman

and

R. Nash Newton

International Language Centre (London) Ltd

Hodder & Stoughton

A MEMBER OF THE HODDER HEADLINE GROUP

British Library Cataloguing in Publication Data

Coleman, Lavinia
  Teach yourself Arabic phrase-book.
  1. Arabic language – Conversation and phrase books
  I. Title   II. Newton, R. Nash   III. Verlande, Aida Zerlande
  492'.7'.83421   PJ6309

ISBN 0 340 23691 4

First published 1980
Seventh impression 1988
Reissued 1992
Impression number   20   19   18   17   16   15   14   13   12
Year   1999   1998   1997   1996   1995

Printed in Great Britain for Hodder & Stoughton Educational, a division
of Hodder Headline Plc, 338 Euston Road, London NW1 3BH by Cox &
Wyman Ltd, Reading, Berks.

Contents

Background

The Language

1. Arabic is a semitic language. It is written from right to left.
2. Arabic is the language of the 'Qur'aan'.
3. Arabic is spoken by over one hundred million Arabs in twenty countries and serves as the language of religion in twenty-nine Islamic countries.
4. Throughout the Arab World written classical Arabic is unified and serves as a *Lingua Franca*.
5. Spoken Arabic differs considerably from country to country and even from district to district.
6. This book attempts to strike a balance by adopting a simplified form of classical Arabic, somewhat freed of tight grammatical restrictions yet comprehensible throughout the Arab World. This is the trend recently followed by the Arab mass media (especially television and radio) to reach the widest possible audience.

7.   Most Arabic letters take different forms according to whether they are initial, medial or terminal.

8.   The short vowels (a, u, i), represented by signs above or below the letter in Arabic, appear in the transliteration but are omitted in the Arabic script.

9.   The phrases in this book are given in the masculine singular. Where applicable, the feminine singular appears after the word or phrase and marked by an oblique *e.g.* **min faDlak 'imla'/min faDlik 'imla'y**.

10.   Do not hesitate to resort to gestures and facial expressions as they are abundantly used by Arab speakers.

11.   In cases where misunderstanding might arise, alternative Arabic words appear in brackets for the English meaning.

12.   In cases of severe difficulty (*e.g.* laryngitis/deafness) show the Arabic script!

13.   An asterisk * on the left of the phrase means that this is a phrase you will need to understand but not to say yourself, *e.g.* 'Have you got anything to declare?'

The culture

1.   The Middle East is the cradle of ancient civilisations. Here you can find the records of Sumerian, Babylonian, Pharaonic, Greek, Phoenician, Roman, Byzantine, Islamic and Ottoman civilisations. There is a wealth of history to be seen.

2.   Hospitality is second nature to the Arabs. You find yourself a welcome guest in Arab homes. You are likely to be pressed to overeat but your host will understand if you insist on refusing.

3.   Greetings are always followed by inquiry about your affairs and health and the health of every member of your household (the concern is genuine).

Compliments are not only welcome but also expected.

There are clichés for every occasion in Arabic. It would be worth learning some and using them at the proper time and place.

4. Go armed with information on colleges and institutes at home. Most young people you meet are interested in education abroad and would ask your advice.

5. When visiting offices expect to be offered frequent cups of tea and coffee.

6. In restaurants, tipping is expected even where service is included in the bill.

7. Bargaining in the sooks is common practice. Big stores usually have fixed prices.

8. When changing currency, shop around for a good rate.

9. There is a wide range of souvenirs to take home: brass, cabinet work, pottery, needlework, wooden backgammon sets inlaid with shells, cedarwood souvenirs, antiques, fossils and, of course, jewellery.

The alphabet

Arabic Letter	Symbol	Description
ء	'	Glottal stop. Like that before the vowel in 'OH'.
ب	b	As in 'bet'.
ت	t	Dental as in 'till'.
ث	th	As in 'thin'.
ج	j	Like the j sound in 'vision' or the French 'je'.

ح	**H**	Unvoiced pharyngeal fricative. Strong expulsion of breath, almost the same as the sound produced while blowing on spectacles to clean them.
خ	**kh**	As in Scottish 'loch'.
د	**d**	As in 'dim'.
ذ	**dh**	As in 'then'.
ر	**r**	As in 'run'.
ز	**z**	As in 'zinc'.
س	**s**	As in 'sit'.
ش	**sh**	As in 'shoe'.
ص	**S**	Emphatic velarised form of 's'. Almost like the s in 'Sum'.
ض	**D**	Emphatic velarised form of 'd'. Almost like the d in 'dumb'.
ط	**T**	Emphatic velarised form of 't'. Almost like the t in 'tar'.
ظ	**Z**	Emphatic velarised form of 'z'. Almost like the z in 'Czar'.
ع	**9**	Voiced pharyngeal fricative. Can be re-produced by pressing the back of the tongue down and saying 'aaaah'. Nine without the first 'n' gives the name of this letter '-ine'.
غ	**gh**	Like the Parisian 'r'.

ف	f	As in 'off' not 'of'.
ق	q	Like the 'k' sound but produced further back in the throat.
ك	k	As in 'king' and 'cat'.
ل	l	As in 'long'.
م	m	As in 'moon'.
ن	n	As in 'neat'.
ه	h	As in 'hang'.
و	w	As in 'wet'.
ي	y	As in 'yes'.

Short Vowels

◌َ	a	As in 'hat'.
◌ِ	i	As in 'tin'.
◌ُ	u	As in 'put'.

Long vowels

ا	aa	As in 'car' and 'heart'.
ي	ee	As in 'meet'.
و	oo	As in 'mood'.

Diphthongs

| ◌َيْ | ay | As in 'mine' and 'loci'. |
| ◌َوْ | aw | As in 'fowl'. |

Note: In front of words beginning with: t, th, d, dh, r, z, s, sh, S,

D, T, Z, l and n (called the 'sun letters' in Arabic) the 'l' of the definite article 'al' is assimilated to the following consonant, *E.g.* 'al-nawm' becomes 'annawm'.

A General Grammar Guide

Here are a few basic outlines to help you get around in Arabic. It is not intended as a full guide.

Nouns

There is no neuter gender in Arabic. All nouns are either masculine or feminine. While most nouns are of invariable gender, the masculine form of verbal nouns, some proper nouns and names of animals can be changed to feminine by adding 'ah'-.

kaatib (writer) كاتب   **kaatibah** كاتبه

sameer (proper noun) سمير   **sameerah** سميره

hirr (cat) هرّ   **hirrah** هرّه

Verbal nouns are derived from verbs. If they end in 'ah' they are usually feminine. Some of the derivatives of the verb **'rasama'** (drew) are given as an example:

rasm (drawing) رسم

rusoomaat (drawings) رسومات

rassaam (artist) رسّام

rassaamah (female artist) رسامه

marsam (studio of an artist) مرسم

rasmy (official) رسميّ

risaamah (ordination of a priest) رِسامه

maraasim (ceremonies) مراسِم

marsoom (decree) مرسوم

Plural

There are two types of plural in Arabic:

Plural for two: add 'ayn' to masculine nouns, and 'tayn' to feminine nouns. *E.g.*

rajul (man) رجل **rajulayn** (two men) رجلين

sayyaarah (car) سيّاره **sayyaaratayn** (two cars) سيّارتين

Plural for three or more: is, again, three forms:

1. Sound masculine: add 'een',

>   *E.g.* **fallaaH** (peasant) فلاّح **fallaaHeen** فلاّحين

2. Sound feminine: add 'aat',

E.g. **fallaaHah** فلاّحه **fallaaHaat** فلاّحات

3. Irregular: radical change in the singular,

E.g. **rajul** رجل **rijaal** رجال

Adjectives

In Arabic adjectives follow the noun and they agree in number and gender. To modify a feminine noun, add 'ah' to the masculine adjective. *E.g.*

rajul shaaTir رجل شاطر **'imra'ah shaaTirah** امرأه شاطره
(clever man)   (clever woman)

Pronouns

Pronouns are either 'separate' as in personal pronouns, or suffixes as shown in the following tables and in the section on Verbs.

Personal pronouns

I	**'anaa**	أنا
you	**'anta** (masc. sing.)	أنتَ
	'anti (fem. sing.)	أنتِ
he	**huwa**	هو
she	**hiya**	هي
we	**naHnu**	نحن
you	**'antum** (masc. pl.)	أنتمِ
	'antunna (fem. pl.)	أنتنَ
they	**hum** (masc. pl.)	همِ
	hunna (fem. pl.)	هن

Suffix Pronouns

my, me	**-y**	ي
your, you (obj.)	**-ak** (masc. sing.)	كَ
	-ik (fem. sing.)	كِ
his, him	**-uh**	ـه
her	**-haa**	ها
our, us	**-naa**	نا
your, you (obj.)	**-kum** (masc. pl.)	كُم
	-kunna (fem. pl.)	كُنّ
their, them	**-hum** (masc. pl.)	هُم
	-hunna	هُنّ

Verbs

Verbs agree with the subject in gender and number. This is done by the use of prefixes and suffixes as shown in the example below. Note that the change in tenses changes the short vowel sounds in the verb.

rasama (drew):

Past Tense	*Present Tense*	*Imperative*
rasam-tu	**'a-rsum**	
رسمتُ	أرسم	
rasam-ta	**ta-rsum**	**-'u-rsum**
رسمتَ	ترسم	أرسم

rasam-ti	ta-rsum-een	'u-rsum-y
رَسمتِ	ترسمين	أُرسِمي
rasam-a	ya-rsum	
رسم	يرسم	
rasam-at	ta-rsum	
رسّمت	ترسم	
rasam-naa	na-rsum	
رسّمنا	نرسم	
rasam-tum	ta-rsum-oon	'u-rsum-oo
رسّمُم	ترسمون	أُرسِموا
rasam-tunna	ta-rsum-na	'u-rsum-na
رسّمتن	ترسمنّ	أُرسِمنّ
rasam-oo	ya-rsum-oon	
رسّموا	يرسمون	
rasam-na	ya-rsum-na	
رسّمن	يرسمن	

The future tense is formed by adding another prefix to the present tense. The prefix 'sa' is used for all persons.

E.g. **sa'arsum** (I shall draw).   سأرسم

Everyday Words and Phrases

Everyday words

Here are some useful adjectives and adverbs and their opposites; the more of them you get to know by heart, the more easily you will find you can communicate. In modifying feminine nouns, remember to add (**ah**):

e.g. beautiful girl   **bint jameelah**

For the plural of both genders, refer to 'Grammar Section'. The words marked + + are invariable.

good	**jayyid**	جيّد
bad	**sayyi'**	سيّء
+ +better	**'aHsan**	أحسَن
+ +worse	**'aswa'**	أسوأ
cheap	**rakheeS**	رخيص

expensive	**ghaaly**	غالي
+ +right	**SaHH**	صح
+ +wrong	**khaTa'**	خطأ
big	**kabeer**	كبير
small	**Sagheer**	صغير
hot	**Haarr**	حار
cold	**baarid**	بارد
near	**qareeb**	قريب
far	**ba9eed**	بعيد
early	**mubakkir**	مبكّر
late	**muta'akhkhir**	متأخّر
next	**'attaaly**	التّالي
last	**'al'akheer**	الأخير
open	**maftooH**	مفتوح
closed	**mughlaq**	مغلق
vacant	**faaDy**	فاضي
occupied	**mashghool**	مشغول
easy	**sahl**	سهل
difficult	**Sa9b**	صعب
quick	**saree9**	سريع
slow	**baTee'**	بطيء

full	**mal'aan**	ملآن
empty	**faarigh**	فارغ
heavy	**thaqeel**	ثقيل
light	**khafeef**	خفيف
beautiful	**jameel**	جميل
ugly	**qabeeH**	قبيح
old	**musinn (qadeem)**	مسنّ (قديم)
young	**shaabb**	شاب
new	**jadeed**	جديد
clever	**shaaTir**	شاطر
stupid	**ghabyy**	غبي
ill	**mareeD**	مريض
well	**Hasan**	حسن

A few words which can be used with the preceding adjectives and adverbs:

++ very	**katheer (jiddan)**	كثير (جداً)
++too	**'ayDan (jiddan)**	(أيضا) جداً
++enough	**kifaayah**	كفاية
++more	**'akthar**	أكثر
++less	**'aqall**	أقل

Lastly, a list of words necessary for most sentences, but especially useful for directions and instructions:

in	**fee**	في
to	**'ilaa**	إلى
at	**fee**	في
on	**9alaa**	على
from	**min**	من
of	**min**	من
with	**ma9**	مع
without	**bidoon**	بدون
for	**li'ajl**	لأجل
near	**qurb**	قرب
past (beyond)	**ba9d**	بعد
next to	**bijaanib**	بجانب
behind	**waraa'**	وراء
in front of	**'amaam**	أمام
opposite	**muqaabil**	مقابل
(a)round	**Hawl**	حول
over	**fawq**	فوق
above	**fawq**	فوق
before (time)	**qabl**	قبل

after (time)	**ba9d**	بعد
after (place)	**ba9d**	بعد
under	**taHt**	تحت

Useful phrases

Greetings

Good morning.   **SabaaH 'alkhayr**

صباح الخير .

Good evening.   **massa' 'alkhayr**

مساء الخير .

Good night.   **tiSbaH/tiSbaHy 9alaa khayr**

تصبح على خير .

Goodbye.   **ma9 'assalaamah**

مع السلامه .

See you.   **'araak/araaky**

اراك .

–this evening.   **haadhaa 'almasaa'**

هذا المساء .

–tomorrow.   **ghadan**

غدًا .

–this afternoon.   **ba9d 'aZZuhr**

بعد الظهر .

–later.   **ba9dayn**

بعدين

Anywhere

Yes.	**na9am**
	نعم
No.	**laa**
	لا
Thank you.	**shukran**
	شكرًا .
Thank you very much.	**shukran jazeelan**
	شكرًا جزيلاً .
Please.	**min faDlak/faDlik**
	من فضلك .
Of course/surely.	**Tab9an/min kull budd**
	طبعًا / من كل بد .
Excuse me, may I?	**9afwan tismaHly/tismaHeely**
	عفوًا تسمحلي ؟
It's very kind of you.	**haadhaa min luTfak/luTfik**
	هذا من لطفك .
What did you say?	**maadhaa qult/qulty**
	ماذا قلت ؟
I'm very sorry.	**'anaa muta'assif/muta'assifah jiddan**
	أنا متأسّف جدًا .
I beg your pardon.	**'arjook/'arjooky 'assamaaH**
	أرجوك السّماح .

That's all right.

ma9laysh

معليش .

Never mind.

laa tahtamm/tahtammy

لا تهتم .

Language problems

I don't understand.

'anaa la 'afham

أنا لا أفهم .

Do you speak English?

hal tatakallamy 'ingleezy

هل تتكلّم إنجليزي ؟

Does anyone here speak
English?

fee 'aHad hunaa yatakallam
'ingleezy

في أحد هنا يتكلّم إنجليزي ؟

Please speak more
slowly.

min faDlak takallam/faDlik
takallamy bibuT' 'akthar

من فضلك تكلّم ببطء اكثر .

What does ... mean?

maa ma9na

ما معنى . . . ؟

Could you translate
this, please?

mumkin tutarjim/tutarjimy
haadhaa min faDlak/faDlik

ممكن تترجم هذا من فضلك ؟

Yes, I understand.

na9am 'anaa 'afham

نعم أنا أفهم .

Questions

Where is ... ?	'ayn
	أين . . . ؟
Where are ... ?	'ayn
	أين . . . ؟
What time is it?	kam 'assaa9ah
	كم الساعه ؟
What is this?	maa haadhaa
	ما هذا ؟
When is ... ?	mataa
	متى . . . . ؟
How much is ... ?	kam si9r...
	كم سعر . . . . ؟
How far is ... ?	kam yab9ud ...
	كم يبعد . . . . ؟
How long does ... take?	kam ya'khudh ... min 'alwaqt'
	كم يأخذ . . . من الوقت ؟
How?	kayf
	كيف ؟
Who?	mann
	من
Why?	limaadhaa
	لماذا ؟

Why not?	**lima laa**
	لمَ لا ؟
What do you want?	**maadhaa tureed**
	ماذا تريد ؟
What's the matter?	**maa 'alkhabar**
	ما الخبر ؟

All the necessary questions will be given in full in all the situations where they might occur.

Meeting people

How do you do?	**keef Haalak/Haalik**
	كيف حالك ؟
I'm pleased to meet you.	**tasharrafhaa**
	تشرفنا
How are you?	**keefak/keefik**
	كيفك ؟
Very well thank you.	**jayyid jiddan, shukran**
	جيد جدًا شكرًا .
This is	**haadhaa**
	هذا . . .
– Mr …	**'assayyid**
	السيد . . .
– Mrs …	**'assayyidah**
	السيده . . .

– Miss ...	**'al'aanisah**
	الآنسه . . .
How is ...?	**keef**
	كيف . . . ؟

Small talk

Here are a few phrases and questions to help you meet and talk to people on a social level:

Hello.	**marHabaa**
	. مرجبا
What's your name?	**maa 'ismak/ismik**
	ما إسمك ؟
I'm English.	**'anaa 'ingleezy/'ingleeziyyah**
	. أنا إنجليزي
Where do you come from?	**min 'ayn 'anta/'anty**
	من أين أنت ؟
Do you like it here?	**hal 'anta masroor hunaa/'anty masroorah**
	هل أنت مسرور هنا ؟
I like.	**'anaa 'uHibb**
	أنا أحب
I don't like.	**'anaa laa 'uHibb**
	. أنا لا أحب

Have you got a light, please?

9indak/9indik wal9ah min faDlak/faDlik

عندك ولعة من فضلك ؟

Do you smoke?

hal tudakhkhin/tudakhkhiny

هل تدخّن ؟

Would you like ....

hal tuHibb tuHibby

هل تحب . . . .

– a drink?

ka's mashroob

كأس مشروب ؟

– a cigarette?

seegaarah

سيجاره ؟

– a coffee?

finjaan qahwah

فنجان قهوه ؟

– to dance?

'an tarquS/tarquSy

أن ترقص ؟

– to go out tonight?

'an takhruj/takhrujy 'allaylah

أن تخرج الليله ؟

– to go to the discotheque?

'an tadhhab/tadhhaby 'ilaa 'almarqaS

أن تذهب إلى المرقص ؟

I'm hungry.

'anaa joo9aan/joo9aanah

أنا جوعان .

I'm thirsty.	**'anaa 9aTshaan/9aTshaanah**
	أنا عطشان .
I'm tired.	**'anaa ta9baan/ta9baanah**
	أنا تعبان .
Yes, please.	**na9am min faDlak/faDlik**
	نعم من فضلك .
No, thank you.	**laa, shukran**
	لا شكرًا .
Can we meet again?	**hal naqdir 'an naltaqy marrah thaaniyah**
	هل نقدر أن نلتقي مرة ثانيه ؟
When?	**mataa**
	متي ؟
See you again soon.	**'araak/'araaky marrah thaaniyah qareeban**
	أراك مره ثانيه قريبا .
Hope to see you again soon.	**'aamal 'an'araak/araaky marrah thaaniyah qareeban**
	آمل أن أراك مره ثانيه قريبا .
What a pity.	**yaa khasaarah**
	يا خساره .
Tomorrow.	**ghadan**
	غدًا .
– morning.	**SabaaHan**
	صباحًا .

– afternoon.   **ba9d 'aZZuhr**

بعد الظهر .

– evening.   **masaa'an**

مساءً .

Goodbye.   **ma9 'assalaamah**

مع السلامه .

The weather

What's the weather going   **kayf sayakoon 'aTTaqs**
to be like?

كيف سيكون الطقس ؟

– today?   **'alyawm**

اليوم ؟

– tomorrow?   **ghadan**

غدًا ؟

– this afternoon?   **ba9d 'aZZuhr**

بعد الظهر ؟

Is it going to rain?   **hal satumTir**

هل ستمطر ؟

Is it going to be fine?   **hal sayakoon Hasan**

هل سيكون حسن ؟

Is it going to snow?   **hal sayanzil thalj**

هل سينزل ثلج ؟

How long is this weather going to last?	**kam sayaTool haadhaa 'aTTaqs** كم سيطول هذا الطقس ؟
Is it going to be hotter/colder?	**hal satazeed 'alHaraarah/ 'alburoodah** هل ستزيد الحراره / البروده ؟
Is the weather going to change?	**hal sayataghayyar 'aTTaqs** هل سيتغير الطقس ؟
It's ... today, isn't it?	**'aTTaqs ... 'alyawm, 'alaysa kadhaalik** الطقس . . . اليوم أليس كذلك ؟
– cold	**baarid** بارد .
– hot	**Haar** حار .
– lovely	**jameel** جميل .
What terrible weather	**maa 'afZa9 'aTTaqs** ما أفظع الطقس .
What lovely weather	**maa 'ajmal 'aTTaqs** ما أجمل الطقس .

On Arrival

Questions you may be asked and the answers you may need.

Customs and passport control

*Have you anything to declare?

hal ma9ak/ma9ik shay' yajib 'an tuSarriH/tuSarriHy bihi?

هل معك شىء يجب أن تصرح به ؟

No, nothing.

laa, laa shay'

لا ، لا شىء

Yes.

na9am

نعم .

*How much money do you have with you?

kam ma9ak/ma9ik fuloos

كم معك فلوس ؟

*How long do you intend
to stay?

**maa muddat
ziyaaratak/ziyaaratik**

ما مدة زيارتك ؟

*Where is your visa?

’ayn ta’sheeratak/sheeratik

أين تأشيرتك ؟

How to get to where you're staying

Where is the luggage
from flight number ...?

**’ayn ’alHaqaa’ib min
’arriHlah raqm**

أين الحقائب من الرحله
رقم . . . . ؟

My bags aren't here.

Haqaa’iby laysat hunaa

حقائبي ليست هنا .

Where is the bureau
de change?

’ayn ’aSSarraaf

أين الصرّاف ؟

Please change this into
...

**min faDlak ’uSruf/faDlik
’uSrufy haadhaa ’almablagh
’ilaa**

من فضلك أصرف هذا المبلغ
إلى . . . . .

Where can I hire a car?

’ayn mumkin ’asta’jir sayyaarah

أين ممكن أستأجر سياره ؟

Where is the bus to the town centre?	'ayn 'albaaS 'ilaa wasaT 'almadeenah
	أين الباص إلى وسط المدينه ؟
Where can I get a taxi?	'ayn mumkin 'ajid taksy
	أين ممكن أجد تاكسي ؟
Please take me to Hotel Sunshine.	min faDlak khudhny 'ilaa funduq sanshayn
	من فضلك خذني إلى فندق سنشاين .
How much is it?	kam 'al'ujrah
	كم الأجره ؟
Where do I get the ... to ... ?	'ayn 'aakhudh 'al ... 'ilaa
	أين آخذ الـ . . . إلى . . . ؟
– train	qiTaar
	قطار .
– bus	baaS
	باص .
– tram	traam
	ترام .
*The ... is over there.	'al ... hunaak
	ألـ . . . هناك .
– station	maHaTTah
	محطة .

– bus stop

mawqif 'albaaS

موقف الباص .

– tram stop

mawqif 'attraam

موقف الترام .

– taxi rank

mawqif 'attaksy

موقف التاكسي .

When's the next bus/
train to ....

**mataa maw9id 'albaaS
('alqiTaar) 'attaaly 'ilaa.**

متى موعد الباص / القطار التالي
إلى . . . . ؟

At the Hotel

Checking in

*Good morning.

SabaaH 'alkhayr

صباح الخير .

*Good evening.

masaa' 'alkhayr

مساء الخير .

*Can I help you?

mumkin 'asaa9idak/'asaa9idik

ممكن أساعدك ؟

*What is your name?

ma 'ismak/'ismik

ما اسمك ؟

My name is ....

'ismy

اسمي . . . .

I have a reservation.

9indy Hajz

عندي حجز .

I haven't got a reservation.	**maa 9indy Hajz** ما عندي حجز .
*How long do you want to stay?	**ma muddat ziyaaratak/ ziyaaratik** ما مده زيارتك ؟
*Please fill this form.	**min faDlak 'imla'/faDlik 'imla'y haadhih 'albiTaaqah** من فضلك إملأ هذه البطاقه .
*Please give me your passport.	**min faDlak/faDlik 'a9Teeny jawaaz safarak/safarik** من فضلك أعطيني جواز سفرك .
I want to stay for	**'ureed 'an 'abqaa muddat** أريد أن أبقى مده . . . .
Have you any vacancies?	**9indakum ghuraf faarighah** عندكم غرف فارغه ؟
Have you a single room?	**9indakum ghurfah mufradah** عندكم غرف مفرده ؟
Have you a double room?	**9indakum ghurfah muzdawijah** عندكم غرمه مزدوجه ؟
With a bath.	**ma9 Hammaam** مع حمّام .
Without a bath.	**bidoon Hammaam** بدون حمّام .

With a shower.	ma9 doosh
	مع دوش .
Have you half board?	9indakum niSf 'alwajbaat
	عندكم نصف الوجبات ؟
– full board?	kul 'alwajbaat
	كل الوجبات ؟
– just bed and breakfast?	sareer wa fuToor faqaT
	سرير وفطور فقط ؟
Can I have a room ...?	mumkin 'aakhudh ghurfah
	ممكن اخذ غرفه . . . ؟
– with a double bed?	bisareer muzdawij
	بسرير مزدوج ؟
– with twin beds?	bisareerayn
	بسريرين ؟
– with a view of the sea?	muTillah 9alaa 'albaHr
	مطله على البحر ؟
– with a wash-basin?	ma9 mighsalah
	مع مغسله ؟
– on the ground floor?	fee 'aTTaabiq 'al'arDy
	في الطابق الأرضي ؟
– on the first floor?	fee 'aTTaabiq 'al'awwal
	في الطابق الأول ؟

– on the second floor?

fee 'aTTaabiq 'aththaany

في الطابق الثاني ؟

Can I see the room first, please?

mumkin 'araa 'alghurfah 'awwalan min faDlak/faDlik

ممكن أرى الغرفه أولاً من فضلك ؟

Can we have a cot for the child/baby?

mumkin ta9Toonaa sareer liTTifl

ممكن تعطونا سرير للطفل ؟

Do we pay extra for it?

hal nadfa9 ziyaadah 9alayh

هل ندفع زياده عليه ؟

How much does it cost ...

kam yukallif

كم يكلّف . . . .

– per night?

fee 'allaylah 'alwaaHidah

في الليله الواحده ؟

– per week?

fee 'al'usboo9

في الأسبوع ؟

Yes, I'll take it.

na9am sa'aakhudhuhaa

نعم آخذها .

No, I won't take it.

laa, lan 'aakhudhuhaa

لا لن سآخذها .

It's too small.

hiya Sagheerah jiddan

هي صغيرة جداً .

It's too dark.   hiya muZlimah jiddan

هي مظلمه جداً .

General
Where is ....   'ayn

أين . . . .

– the car park?   mawqif 'assayyaaraat

موقف السيّارات ؟

– the lift?   'almiS9ad

المصعد ؟

– the dining-room?   ghurfat 'aTTa9aam

غرفة الطعام ؟

– the bar?   'albaar

البار ؟

– the lavatory?   'almirHaaD

المرحاض ؟

– the bathroom?   'alHammaam

الحمّام ؟

– the lounge?   ghurfat 'aljuloos

غرفة الجلوس ؟

– the hairdresser?   'alHallaq

الحلاّق ؟

What time is ....   fee 'ay waqt

في أي وقت . . . .

– breakfast served?

yuqaddam 'alfuToor

يقدّم الفطور ؟

– lunch served?

yuqaddam 'alghadhaa'

يقدّم الغذاء ؟

– dinner served?

yuqaddam 'al9ashaa'

يقدّم العشاء ؟

Room service, please.

khidmat 'alghuraf min faDlak/ faDlik

خدمة الغرف من فضلك .

Can I have breakfast in my room, please?

mumkin 'aakhudh 'alfuToor fee ghurfaty min faDlak/faDlik?

ممكن أخذ الفطور في غرفتي من فضلك ؟

– coffee

qahwah

قهوه .

– tea

shaay

شاي .

At the reception desk

Can I have my key, please?

mumkin 'aakhudh muftaaHy min faDlak/faDlik

ممكن آخذ مفتاحى من فضلك ؟

I've lost my key.

'aDa9t muftaaHy

أضعت مفتاحي .

Please call me at . . . tomorrow.	min faDlak 'ittaSil/faDlik 'ittaSily/bee 'assaa9ah . . . ghadan

من فضلك إتصّلٍ بي
الساعه . . . غداً .

Are there any letters for me?	hal min makaateeb lee

هل من مكاتيب لي ؟

– messages?	rasaa'il

رسائل ؟

The light doesn't work.	'aDDaw' laa yashtaghil

الضوء لا يشتغل .

The air-conditioning	'almukayyif

المكيّف .

The razor socket	kubs 'aalat 'alHilaaqah

كبس اله الحلاقه .

The heating	'attadfi'ah

التدفئه .

The radio	'arraadyu

الراديو .

The lock	'alqifl

القفل .

There's no hot water.	laa yoojad maa' Haar

لا يوجد ماء حار .

– electricity	kahrabaa'

كهرباء .

When someone knocks at the door

Come in.	**'udkhul/udkhuly**

أدخل

Please wait a moment.	**min faDlak 'intaZir/faDlik 'intaZiry laHZah**

من فضلك إنتظر لحظه .

Please come back later.	**min faDlak 'irja9/faDlik 'irja9y ba9dayn**

من فضلك إرجع بعدين .

If you need something

Please bring me	**min faDlak/faDlik 'a9Teeny**

من فضلك أعطيني . . . .

– a towel.	**minshafah**

منشفه .

– a blanket.	**baTTaaniyah (Hiraam)**

بطانيه (حرام) .

– a pillow.	**mikhaddah**

مخده .

– an ashtray.	**minfaDah**

منفضه .

– some coathangers.	**9allaaqaat liththiyaab**

علاقات للثياب .

– some soap.	**Saaboon**

صابون .

– needle and cotton.

'ibrah wa khayT

إبره وخيط .

I'd like room service,
please.

'ureed khidmat 'alghuraf min
faDlak/faDlik

أريد خدمه الغرف من فضلك .

At reception on leaving
Please give me the bill.

min faDlak/faDlik
'9Teeny 'alfaatoorah

من فضلك أعطيني الفاتوره .

What's this entry on the
bill?

maa haadhaa 'arraqm fee
'alfaatoorah

ما هذا الرقم في للفاتوره ؟

Is service included in the
total?

hal 'alkhidmah maHsoobah fee
'almajmoo9

هل الخدمه محسوبه في المجموع ؟

Can I have a receipt?

mumkin 'aakhudh waSl

ممكن آخذ وصل ؟

Here is my home address.

haadhaa 9unwaan bayty

هذا عنوان بيتي .

Here is my forwarding
address.

haadhaa 9unwaany 'attaaly

هذا عنواني التالي .

I'm leaving this
afternoon/tomorrow.

'anaa taarik/taarikah ba9d
'aZZuhr/ghadan

أنا تارك بعد الظهر / غداً .

Could you order a taxi
for ... o'clock?

**mumkin taTlub/taTluby taksy
lissaa9ah**

ممكن تطلب تاكسي
للساعه . . . . ؟

Please could someone
bring my bags down?

**min faDlak/faDlik
mumkin waaHad yunazzil
Haqaa'iby**

من فضلك ممكن واحد ينزل
حقائبي ؟

Camping and Caravanning

Where's the nearest	'ayn 'aqrab
	أين أقرب . . . .
– camp site?	mawqi9 mukhayyam
	موقع مخيّم ؟
– caravan site?	mawqi9 'almaqTooraat 'assakaniyyah
	موقع المقطورات السكنيه ؟
– youth hostel?	nazl lishshabaab
	نزل للشباب ؟
How much is it?	kam yukallif
	كم يكلّف ؟
– per night?	fee 'allaylah
	في الليله ؟

– per week?	fee 'al'usboo9
	في الأسبوع ؟
Are there	hal yoojad
	هل يوجد . . . .
– lavatories?	maraaHeeD?
	مراحيض ؟
– washing facilities?	tasheelaat lilghaseel
	تسهيلات للغسيل ؟
– telephones?	talifoonaat
	تلفونات ؟
Is there	hal yoojad
	هل يوجد . . . .
– a shop?	dukkaan
	دكان ؟
– a launderette?	dukkaan lighasl 'aththiyaab fee ghassaalaat bil'ujrah
	دكان لغسل الثياب في غسّلات بالأجرة ؟
– a restaurant?	maT9am
	مطعم ؟
– a bar?	baar
	بار ؟
– a camping supplies shop?	dukkan lilawaazim 'almukhayyam
	دكان للوازم المخيّم ؟

How far is it from …?   **kam tab9ud 9an**

كم تبعد عن . . . . ؟

VOCABULARY

tent	**khaymah**	خيمة
tent-pole	**9aamood 'alkhaymah**	عامود الخيمة
tent-pegs	**'awtaad lilkhaymah**	أوتاد للخيمه
groundsheet	**sijjaadah li'arD 'alkhaymah**	سجاده لأرض الخيمه
sleeping-bag	**kees linnawm**	كيس للنوم
camp-bed	**sareer mukhayyam**	سرير مخيم
air-mattress	**firash hawaa'y**	فراش هوائي
Primus stove	**waaboor primus**	وابور بريموس
camping-gas	**ghaaz lilmukhayyam**	غاز للمخيم
gas-light	**miSbaaH ghaaz**	مصباح غاز
tool-kit	**Sandooq ma9addaat**	صندوق معدات
first aid kit	**Sandooq 'is9aaf**	صندوق إسعاف
torch	**miSbaaH kahrabaa'y**	مصباح كهربائي
rope	**Habl**	حبل
matches	**kabreet**	كبريت
tin-opener	**fattaaHat 9ulab**	فتّاحه علب
bottle-opener	**fattaaHat qanaany**	فتّاحه قناني

Youth Hostelling

Where's the nearest youth hostel

'ayn 'aqrab nazl lishshabaab

أين أقرب نزل للشباب ؟

I'd like to stay here

'uHibb 'an 'anzil hunaa

أحب أن أنزل هنا .

– for one night.

laylah waaHidah

ليله واحده .

– for two nights.

laylatayn

ليلتين .

*I'm afraid we haven't any room.

'akhshaa 'an laa yakoon 9indanaa ghurfah

أخشى أن لا يكون عندنا غرفة

*Show me your
international youth
hostelling card.

mumkin 'araa biTaaqatak/
biTaaqatik limanaazil
'ashshabaab 'addawliyah

ممكن أرى بطاقتك لمنازل الشباب
الدولية .

*You can only stay one
night.

mumkin tabqqa/tabqay laylah
waaHidah faqat

ممكن تبقي ليله واحده فقط .

I'd like a ....

'ureed

أريد . . . .

– sleeping bag.

kees linnawm

كيس للنوم .

– blanket.

Hiraam (baTTaaniyah)

حرام (بطانيه) .

– a pillow.

mikhaddah

مخده

– a packed lunch.

ghadhaa' fee 9ulbah

غذاء في علبه .

– some hot water.

maa' Haar

ماء حار .

Where's the ....

'ayn

أين . . . .

– kitchen?

'almaTbakh

المطبخ ؟

– bathroom?	'alHammaam
	الحمّام ؟
– shower-room?	'addoosh
	الدوش ؟
Where are the wash-basins?	'ayn 'almaghaasil
	أين المغاسل ؟
What time must we be out in the morning?	'ay waqt yajib 'an nakhruj fee 'aSSabaaH
	أي وقت يجب أن نخرج في الصباح ؟
What time can we come in the evening?	'ay waqt mumkin 'an na9ood fee 'almasaa'
	أي وقت ممكن أن نعود في المساء ؟
What time must we be in at night?	'ayn 'ghayr hunaa, mumkin hunaa fee 'allayl
	أي وقت يجب أن نكون هنا في الليل ؟
Do you give meals here?	hal tuqaddimoon wajbaat hunaa
	هل تقدمون وجبات هنا ؟
Where else can we stay cheaply?	'ayn 'ghayr hunaa, mumkin najid makaan rakheeS
	أين ، غير هنا ، ممكن نجد مكان رخيص ؟

Where is that?	'ayn dhaalik
	أين ذلك ؟
Where can I leave my	'ayn mumkin 'atruk
	أين ممكن أترك . . . .
– bags?	Haqaa'iby
	حقائبي ؟
– rucksack?	'aljurbandiyyah
	الجربنديه ؟
– bicycle?	darraajaty
	درّاجتي ؟

USEFUL SIGNS

ممنوع الدخول .

No entry	mamnoo9 'addukhool

ممنوع دخول السيّارات .

No entry for motor vehicles	mamnoo9 dukhool 'assayyaaraat

ملك خاص

Private property	mulk khaaS

المخالف تتخذ ضده الإجراءات الرسميّة .

Trespassers will be prosecuted	'almukhaalif tuttakhadh Diddahu 'al'ijraa'aat 'arrasmiyyah

No caravans

ممنوع للمقطورات السكنيّه

mamnoo9 lilmaqTooraat 'assakaniyyah

Camping forbidden

ممنوع التخييم

mamnoo9 'attakhyeem

Drinking water

ماء شرب

maa' shurb

Not drinking water

ماء غير صالح للشرب

maa' ghayr SaaliH lishshurb

Travelling

At the mainline station

I'd like a single/return
ticket to ...

'ureed tadhkarah dhahaab/
dhahaab wa 'iyaab 'ilaa

أريد تذكرة ذهاب / ذهاب

وإياب إلى . . . .

*First or second class?

darajah 'oolah 'aw thaaniyah

درجه أولى أو ثانية ؟

What's the single/return
fare?

kam 'ujrat 'adhdhahaab/
'adhdhahaab wa 'al'iyaab

كم أجره الذهاب / الذهاب

والإياب ؟

What's the fare for a
child?

kam thaman tadhkarat 'aTTifl

كم ثمن تذكرة الطفل ؟

Can I reserve a seat?	mumkin 'aHjiz miq9ad
	ممكن أحجز مقعد ؟
I'd like a seat	'ureed miq9ad
	أريد مقعد . . . .
– in a smoking compartment.	fee maqSoorah lilmudakhkhineen
	في مقصوره للمدخّنين
– in a no-smoking compartment.	fee maqSoorah lighayr 'almudakhkhineen
	في مقصورة لغير المدخّنين .
– facing the front.	muwaajih lilmuqaddimah
	مواجه للمقدّمة .
– with my back to the engine.	wa Zahry lilmuHarrik
	وظهري للمحرّك .
Is there ...	hal yoojad
	هل يوجد . . . .
– a buffet-car on the train?	miqSaf fee 'alqiTaar
	مقصف في القطار ؟
– a restaurant-car on the train?	maT9am fee 'alqiTaar
	مطعم في القطار ؟
Is it a sleeper?	hal yoojad 9arabaat nawm
	هل يوجد عربات نوم ؟

I'd like to reserve a berth.	'ureed 'an 'aHjiz sareer
	أريد أن أحجز سرير .
What time does the train leave?	fee 'ay waqt yughaadir 'alqiTaar
	في أي وقت يغادر القطار ؟
– arrive?	yaSil
	يصل ؟
Which platform does it leave from?	min 'ay raSeef yughaadir
	من أي رصيف يغادر ؟
– come in?	yadkhul
	يدخل ؟
Do I have to change trains?	hal yajib 'an 'antaqil min qiTaar 'ilaa 'aakhar
	هل يجب أن أنتقل من قطار إلى آخر ؟
Where?	'ayn
	أين ؟
What time is the connection for ...?	maa maw9id 'alqiTaar 'almoowaaSil 'ilaa
	ما موعد القطار المواصل إلى . . . . ؟
Does this train go to ...?	hal yadhhab haadhaa 'alqiTaar 'ilaa
	هل يذهب هذا القطار إلى . . . . ؟

When's the first/last train to ...?	maa maw9id 'awwal/'aakhir qiTaar 'ilaa.

ما موعد أول / آخر قطار إلى . . . ؟

Have you got a timetable, please?	9indakum jadwal mawaa9eed 'alqiTaaraat min faDlak/faDlik

عندكم جدول مواعيد القطارات من فضلك ؟

Where is	'ayn

أين . . . .

– platform X?	raSeef X

رصيف X ؟

– the waiting-room?	ghurfat 'al'intiZaar

غرفة الانتظار ؟

– the bar?	'albaar

البار ؟

– the information office?	maktab 'al'isti9laamaat

مكتب الاستعلامات ؟

STATIONS SIGNS

المغادرون .

Departures	'almughaadiroon

الوصول

Arrivals	'alwuSool

الحقائب المتروكه .

Left luggage	'alHaqaa'ib 'almatrookah

الرصيف ×

Platform X — 'arraSeef X

المفقودات

Lost property — 'almafqoodaat

الاستعلامات

Information — 'al'isti9laamaat

مكتب التذاكر

Ticket office — maktab 'attadhaakir

الحجز

Reservations — 'alHajz

المراحيض

Lavatories — 'almaraaHeeD

المغاسل

Wash-room — 'almaghaasil

للسيدات .

Ladies — lissayyidaat

للرجال

Gents — lirrijaal

للعائلات

Families — lil9aa'ilaat

غرفة الانتظار

Waiting-room — ghurfat 'al'intiZaar

المقصف

Buffet — 'almiqSaf

Restaurant	المطعم 'almaT9am
Bar	البار 'albaar

On the underground

Which line goes to ...?	'ay khaT yadhhab 'ilaa أي خط يذهب إلى . . . . ؟
Does this train go to ...?	hal yadhhab haadhaa 'alqiTaar 'ilaa هل يذهب هذا القطار إلى . . . . ؟
Where do I change for ...?	'ayn 'ughayyir 'ilaa أين أغير إلى . . . . ؟

On the bus

Where do I get a bus to ...?	'ayn 'aakhudh 'albaaS 'ilaa أين آخذ الباص إلى . . . . ؟
How long does it take?	kam ya'khudh min 'alwaqt كم يأخذ من الوقت ؟
Do I have to change?	hal yajib 'an 'ughayyir هل يجب أن أغير؟

Does this bus go to ...?	**hal yadhhab haadhaa 'albaaS 'ilaa**
	هل يذهب هذا الباص إلى . . . . ؟
How often do they run?	**maa fatrat 'alwaqt bayn 'albaaS wa 'albaaS 'attaaly**
	ما فترة الوقت بين الباص والباص التالي ؟
Please, tell me when to get off?	**min FaDlak qul lee mataa 'anzil**
	من فضلك قل لي متى أنزل ؟
I want to get off at ...	**'ureed 'an 'anzil fee**
	أريد أن أنزل في . . . .

At the airport

English is the most common language at all airports, so you should not normally need to use any phrases in Arabic.

Which gate for flight number ...?	**'ay bawwaabah lirriHlah raqm**
	أي بوابة للرحله رقم . . . . ؟
My bags aren't here.	**Haqaa'iby laysat hunaa**
	حقائبي هنا .

Taxis

I want to go to ... please.

min faDlak 'ureed 'an 'adhhab 'ilaa.

من فضلك أريد أن أذهب
إلى . . . .

How much will it cost to go to ...?

kam 'al'ujrah 'ilaa

كم الأجره إلى . . . . ؟

Could you help me with the bags?

mumkin tusaa9idny fee Haml 'alHaqaa'ib

ممكن تساعدني في حمل الحقائب ؟

I'm in a hurry.

'anaa musta9jil

أنا مستعجل .

Stop here, please.

qif hunaa, min faDlak

قف هنا ، من فضلك .

What's the surcharge for?

kam ziyaadat 'al'ujrah 'ilaa

كم زيادة الأجره إلى ؟

Please wait here for me.

min faDlak 'intaZirny hunaa

من فضلك انتظرني هنا .

Your car

Where is ...

'ayn

أين . . . .

– the next garage?

'algaraaj 'attaaly

الجراج التالي ؟

–the nearest car park?	'aqrab mawqif sayyaaraat أقرب موقف سيارات ؟
–the nearest automatic car wash?	'aqrab ghasl 'utumaateeky أقرب غسل أوتوماتيكي ؟
–the motorway?	'aTTareeq 'arra'eesy الطريق الرئيسي ؟
Can I park here?	mumkin 'ooqif 'assayyaarah hunaa ممكن أوقف السيارة هنا ؟
What does this sign/notice mean?	maadhaa ta9ny haadhih 'al'ishaarah/haadhaa 'al'i9laan ماذا تعني هذه الإشارة / هذا الإعلان ؟
Excuse me, can you tell me the way to ...?	9afwan, mumkin tadullany/ tadulleeny 'aTTareeq 'ilaa عفوا ، ممكن تدلني الطريق إلى . . . . ؟

(for answers see 'Asking the way and Directions' page.

At the Petrol Station
I'd like ten litres of
super, please.

'ureed 9asharat litraat khuSooSy min faDlak

أريد عشرة ليترات خصوصي من فضلك .

–premium, please.	**mumtaaz, min faDlak**
	ممتاز من فضلك .
Please, fill the tank.	**min faDlak 'imla' 'alkhazzaan.**
	من فضلك املأ الخزان .
Please, check....	**min faDlak 'ifHaS**
	من فضلك إفحص . . . .
–the radiator.	**'alraadeeyatur**
	الرادياتور .
–the battery.	**'albaTTaariyyah**
	البطارية .
–the tyre pressure.	**DaghT 'addawaaleeb**
	ضغط الدواليب .
–the oil.	**'azzayt**
	الزيت .
Do you sell cigarettes?	**hal tabee9oon sajaayir**
	هل تبيعون سجاير ؟
–sweets?	**Halwa**
	حلوى ؟
Where is the lavatory please?	**'ayn 'almirHaaD min faDlak**
	أين المرحاض من فضلك ؟

At the garage for repairs etc.
My car has broken down.

sayyaaraty ta9aTTalat

سيارتي تعطّلت .

—won't start.	laa tadoor
	لا تدور .
I've run out of petrol.	khalaS 'albanzeen 9indy
	خلص البنزين عندي .
The carburettor is blocked	'alkarbooratur masdood
	الكاربوراتور مسدود .
The hand brake isn't working.	faraamil 'alyadd laa tashtaghil
	فرامل اليد لا تشتغل .
The foot brake	faraamil 'arrijl.
	فرامل الرجل .
The clutch	'alklatsh ('addubriyaaj)
	الكلتش (الدويرياج) .
The horn	'azzammoor
	الزمّور .
The gears are jammed.	'algeer (veetess) mashbook
	الجير (فيتس) مشبوك .
The starter is jammed.	muftaaH 'almuHarrik mashbook
	مفتاح المحرك مشبوك .
The accelerator	dawwaasat 'albanzeen
	دوّاسة البنزين .
The fan-belt is broken.	qishaaT 'almarwaHah maqToo9
	قشاط المروحة مقطوع .

The windscreen wipers aren't working.	massaaHaat 'azzujaaj laa tashtaghil
	مسّاحات الزجاج لا تشتغل .
The brake lights	Daw' 'alfaraamil
	ضوء الفرامل .
The headlights	'aDDaw' 'al'amaamy
	الضوء الأمامي .
The indicators	Daw' 'al'ishaarah
	ضوء الإشارة .
The rear lights	'aDDaw' 'alkhalfy
	الضوء الخلفي .
Could you recharge the battery?	mumkin tashHan 'albaTTaariyyah
	ممكن تشحن البطّارية ؟
How long will it take to repair?	kam min 'alwaqt ya'khudh 'attaSleeH
	كم من الوقت يأخذ التصليح ؟
How much will it cost?	kam 'alkilfah
	كم الكلفه ؟
I've got ...	9indy
	عندي . . . .
– a puncture	thuqb fee 'addoolaab
	ثقب في الدولاب
– a flat battery	baTTariyyah faarighah
	بطاريه فارغه

–damp spark-plugs	boojee (plakkaat) raTbah
	بوجي (بلكات) رطبه
Have you got ...	9indak
	عندك . . . .
–another tyre?	doolaab 'aakhar
	دولاب آخر ؟
–a can of petrol?	tanakat banzeen
	تنكه بنزين ؟
–a can of oil?	tanakat zayt
	تنكه زيت ؟
–a can of brake fluid?	tanakat zayt faraamil
	تنكه زيت فرامل ؟
–a pressure gauge?	miqyaas liDDaghT
	مقياس للضغط ؟

Hiring a car

I'd like to hire a car, please.	'ureed 'isti'jaar sayyaarah min faDlak
	أريد إستئجار سياره من فضلك
The smallest/largest you have.	'aSghar/'akbar sayyaarah 9indak
	أصغر/أكبر سيارة عندك
A mini.	meeny
	ميني

A saloon	**Saaloon** صالون
A two-door car.	**sayyaarah bibaabayn** سيارة ببابين
A four-door car.	**sayyaarah bi'arba9 'abwaab** سيارة بأربع أبواب
A convertible.	**sayyaarah makshoofah** سيارة مكشوفه
With a sun-roof.	**ma9 saTH shamsy** مع سطح شمسي
For … days.	**li … 'ayyaam** لـ . . . . أيام
For one week.	**li'usboo9 waaHid** لأسبوع واحد
For two weeks.	**li'usboo9ayn** لأسبوعين
Can I hire a car for one day?	**mumkin 'asta'jir sayyaarah liyawm waaHid** ممكن أستأجر سيّارة ليوم واحد ؟
Can I hire a car for the week-end?	**mumkin 'asta'jir sayyaarah li9uTlat nihaayat 'al'usboo9?** ممكن أستأجر سيّارة لعطلة نهاية الأسبوع ؟

Could we have a chauffeur-driven car?	mumkin na'khudh sayyaarah ma9 saa'iq

ممكن نأخذ سيّارة مع سائق ؟

How much does it cost?	kam tukallif

كم تكلّف ؟

Does that include comprehensive insurance?	hal haadhaa yataDamman ta'meen shaamil

هل هذا يتضمن تأمين شامل ؟

Can I return it in a different town?	mumkin 'urajji9haa fee balad 'aakhar

ممكن أرجعها في بلد آخر ؟

Must I bring it back to this office?	laazim 'urajji9haa 'ilaa haadhaa 'almaktab

لازم أرجعها إلى هذا المكتب ؟

Have you got an office in ...?	9indakum maktab fee

عندكم مكتب في . . . . ؟

Is there a deposit?	hal 'adfa9 9urboon

هل أدفع عربون ؟

Can I see the car, please?	mumkin 'araa 'assayyaarah min faDlak

ممكن أرى السيّارة من فضلك ؟

I'd like an automatic, please.	'ureed sayyaarah 'utumateek min faDlak

أريد سيّارة أوتوماتيك من فضلك

Can I have a car manual, please?	**mumkin 'aakhudh kitaab daleel 'assayyaarah min faDlak**

ممكن آخذ كتاب دليل السيّارة من
فضلك ؟

Written road signs

In more rural areas you may still see road-signs written in Arabic and not the international symbols. Here are some of the more usual ones:

قد سيارتك ببطء

Drive slowly	**qud sayyaaratak bibuT'**

قد سيارتك بحذر

Drive carefully	**qud sayyaaratak biHadhar**

خفف السرعه (تمهل)

Slow down	**khaffif 'assur9ah (tamahhal)**

قف

Halt	**qif**

مدرسة

School	**madrasah**

أشغال / عمال يشتغلون

Roadworks	**'ashghaal/9ummaal yashtaghiloon**

إتجاه جبري

Diversion	**'ittijaah jabry**

طريق رئيسي

Motorway	**'otostraad**

Level crossing	تقاطع السكه الحديد والطريق العام taqaaTu9 'assikkah 'alHadeed waTTareeq 'al9aam
Crossroads	مفرق طرق mafraq Turuq
No entry (one-way street)	ممنوع الدخول (السيري إتجاه واحد) mamnoo9 'addukhool ('assayr fee 'ittijaah waaHid)
No parking	ممنوع الوقوف mamnoo9 'alwuqoof
Private road	طريق خاص Tareeq khaaS
Danger	خطر khaTar

Asking the way and directions

Excuse me.	9afwan عفوًا
Can you tell me the way to ...?	mukin tadullany/tadulleeny 'aTTareeq 'ilaa

ممكن تدلني الطريق

Where is ...?	'ayn
	أين . . . . ؟
Is it a long walk?	hal 'almasaafah Taweelah lilmashy
	هل المسافه طويله للمشي ؟
Can I take a bus/train there?	mumkin 'aakhudh baaS/qiTaar 'ilaa hunaak
	ممكن آخذ باص / قطار إلى هناك ؟
Where am I on this map?	'ayn 'anaa 9alaa haadhih 'alkhaariTah
	أين أنا على هذه الخارطه ؟
Where is it on this map?	'ayn hiyaa 9alaa haadhih 'alkhaariTah
	أين هي على هذه الخارطه ؟
*Go back.	'irja9/'irja9y
	إرجع
*Carry straight on.	'imshy dughry (9alaa Tool)
	إمشي دغري (على طول)
*Turn right.	liff/liffy yameen
	لف يمين
*Turn left.	liff/liffy yasaar (shimaal)
	لف يسار (شمال)
*Take the	khudh/khudhy
	خذ . . . .

–first left.	'al'awwal yasaar (shimaal)
	الأول يسار (شمال)
–second.	'aththaany
	الثاني
–third.	'aththaalith
	الثالث
–right/left.	yameen/yasaar (shimaal)
	يمين / يسار (شمال)
–main road.	Tareeq ra'eesy
	طريق رئيسي
*Cross the road.	'iq Ta9/'iqTa9y 'aTTareeq
	إقطع الطريق
*At the traffic light.	9alaa 'ishaarat 'almuroor
	على إشارة المرور
*At the cross-roads.	9alaa mafraq 'aTTuruq
	على مفرق الطرق
*At the cinema.	9ind 'asseenamah
	عند السينما
*Then ask again.	hunaak 'is'al/'is'aly marrah thaaniyah
	هناك إسأل مره ثانيه
*It's right in front of you.	hiyaa 'amaamak 'amaamik biZZabT
	هي أمامك بالضبط

*It's only a short way
from here.

hiyaa 9alaa masaafah
qareebah min hunaa

هي على مسافة قريبة من هنا .

*It's a long way.

'almasaafah ba9eedah.

المسافة بعيدة .

*It's about two streets
from here.

ba9d shaari9ayn min hunaa

بعد شارعين من هنا .

Shopping

Names of shops and places

bakery	**furn (makhbaz)**	فرن (مخبز)
bank	**bank (maSraf)**	بنك (مصرف)
butcher's	**laHHaam**	لحّام
car park	**mawqif sayyaaraat**	موقف سيّارات
chemist	**Saydaliyyah**	صيدليّة
clothes shop	**maHall thiyaab**	محل ثياب
florist	**maHall zuhoor**	محل زهور
grocer	**baqqaal**	بقّال
greengrocer	**baa'i9 khuDrawaat**	بائع خضروات

hairdresser	Hallaq (muzayyin)	حلاق (مزين)
ironmonger	baa'i9 'adawaat wa	بائع أدوات
	ma9addaat	ومعدات
laundry	maSbaghah	مصبغة
police station	makhfar 'ashshurTah	مخفر الشرطة
post office	maktab 'albareed	مكتب البريد
tobacconist	baa'i9 sajaayir	بائع شجاير
barber	Hallaq	حلاق
electrician	kahrabaa'y	كهربائي
supermarket	sooparmaarkit	سوبرماركت

In a food shop

Have you got	9indakum	عندكم ....
–butter?	zibdah	زبدة ؟
–cheese?	jibnah	جبنة ؟
–milk?	Haleeb	حليب ؟
–cold meats?	luHoom baaridah	لحوم باردة ؟

–eggs?	bayD
	بيض ؟
Can I have	mumkin 'aakhudh
	ممكن آخذ ....
–a tin of	9ulbat
	علبة ....
–fruit?	faakihah
	فاكهة ؟
–coffee?	qahwah
	قهوة ؟
–tomatoes?	banadoorah
	بندورة ؟
–a packet of	9ulbat
	علبة ....
–sugar?	sukkar
	سكر ؟
–tea?	shaay
	شاي ؟
–rice?	'aruzz
	أرز ؟
–a loaf of bread?	ragheef khubz
	رغيف خبز ؟
–a bottle of	qanneenat
	قنّينه ....

–milk?	**Haleeb**
	حليب ؟
–fruit juice?	**9aSeer faakihah**
	عصير فاكهة ؟
–beer?	**beerah**
	بيرة ؟
–mineral water?	**maa' ma9daniyyah**
	ماء معدنية ؟
–soda water?	**maa' Soda**
	ماء صودا ؟
–lemonade?	**laymunaaDah**
	ليموناضة ؟
Have you got a box, please?	**9indak/9indik Sandooq, min faDlak/faDlik**
	عندك صندوق من فضلك ؟
Have you got a carrier bag, please?	**9indak/9indik kees kabeer min faDlak/faDlik**
	عندك كيس كبير من فضلك ؟

VOCABULARY

Meat and Fish

lamb	**kharoof (ghanam)**	خروف (غنم)
pork	**khanzeer**	خنزير
veal	**9ijl**	عجل

beef	**baqar**	بقر
steak	**stayk (biftayk)**	ستيك (بفتيك)
liver	**kibd**	كبد
kidneys	**kalaawy**	كلاوي
chop	**kastalaytah**	كستليتة
ham	**haam (jambon)**	هام (جامبون)
sole	**samak moosaa**	سمك موسى
tuna	**Tun**	طون
red mullet	**sulTaan 'ibraaheem**	سلطان إبراهيم
sardine	**sardeen**	سردين
cod	**qudd**	قد
turbot	**samak 'atturs**	سمك الترس
trout	**trawt**	تراوت
shrimps	**quraydis**	قريدس
prawns	**rubyaan (ganbary)**	ربيان (جنبري)

Vegetables and Fruit

a kilo of	**keeloo min**	كيلو من ....
potatoes	**baTaaTaa**	بطاطا
tomatoes	**banadoorah** (Tamaa Tim)	بندورة (طماطم)
lettuce	**khass**	خس

carrots	jazar	جزر
peas	bazillaa	بازيلا
beans	loobiyaa' (faaSoolyah)	لوبياء (فاصوليا)
cabbage	malfoof	ملفوف
apples	tuffaaH	تفّاح
oranges	burtuqaal	برتقال
grapefruit	graypfroot	غريب فروت
grapes	9inab	عنب
melon	shammaam (baTTeekh 'aSfar)	شمام (بطيخ اصفر)
bananas	mawz	موز
peaches	durraaq	دراق
apricots	mishmish	مشمش
strawberries	frayz (faraawlah)	فريز (فراولة)
raspberries	toot shawky (frambwaaz)	توت شوكي (فرامبواز)
watermelon	baTTeekh	بطيخ

At the tobacconist

(For stamps, see 'Post Office' section.)

| Have you got a postcard ... | 9indakum biTaaqah bareediyyah عندكم بطاقة بريدية . . . . |

–of the palace?	lilqaSr
	للقصر ؟
–of the castle?	lilqal9ah
	للقلعة ؟
–of the cathedral?	lilkaathidraa'iyyah
	للكاثدرائية ؟
–of the hotel?	lilfunduq
	للفندق ؟
–of the park?	lilHadeeqah 'al9aamah
	للحديقة العامة ؟
–of the sea?	lilbaHr
	للبحر ؟
Have you got ...?	9indakum
	عندكم . . . . ؟
Please give me a packet of ...	min faDlak/faDlik 'a9Teeny 9ulbat
	من فضلك أعطيني علبة . . . .
–un-tipped cigarettes.	sajaayir bidoon filtar
	سجاير بدون فلتر .
–tipped cigarettes.	sajaayir bifiltar
	سجاير بفلتر .
–cigarillos.	seegaar Sagheer
	سيجار صغير .

–peppermints.	'aqraaS na9na9
	أقراص نعنع
–chewing-gum.	9ilkah
	علكة .
–tobacco (strong/mild/sweet).	tanbaak lilghalyoon (qawy/khafeef/Hiloo)
	تنباك للغليون
	(قوي / خفيف / حلو) .
Please can I have ...	min faDlak/faDlik 'a9Teeny
	من فضلك أعطيني . . . .
–some matches.	kabreet
	كبريت .
–some pipe-cleaners.	munaZZifaat lilghalyoon
	منظفات للغليون .
–a bar of chocolate. (milk/plain)	lawH shukulaaTah (bilHaleeb/saadah)
	لوح شوكولاطة (بالحليب / سادة) .
–a box of chocolates. (bit/small)	9ulbat shukulaaTah (kabeerah/Sagheerah)
	علبة شوكولاطة (كبيرة / صغيرة) .

Smoking

Have a cigarette.	khudh/khudhy seejaarah
	خذ سيجارة .

No, thanks, I don't smoke.   **laa shukran, 'anaa laa
                               'udakhkhin**

لا شكرا ، أنا لا أدخن .

At the chemist

Medical Items
Please give me ...   **min faDlak/faDlik 'a9Teeny**

من فضلك أعطيني . . . .

–some cotton-wool.   **quTn**

قطن .

–some disinfectant.   **muTahhir**

مطهّر .

–some antiseptic cream.   **marham mu9aqqim**

مرهم معقّم .

–some sticking-plaster.   **shareeT laaSiq**

شريط لاصق .

–a bandage.   **rabTah**

ربطة .

–a crepe bandage.   **rabTah maTTaaTah**

ربطة مطاطة .

–some cough medicine.   **dawaa' sa9lah (kuHHah)**

دواء سعلة (كحّة) .

–some throat lozenges.   **'aqraaS lilHalq (lilbul9oom)**

أقراص للحلق (للبلعوم)

—some gargle.	**ghargharah**
	غرغرة .
—some stomach tablets. (anti-diarrhoea)	**'aqraaS/Didd 'al'ishaal**
	أقراص ضد الإسهال .
—some digestive pills.	**'aqraaS muhaDDimah**
	أقراص مهضّمة .
—some laxative.	**mulayyin lilma9idah**
	ملیّن للمعدة .
—some insect repellant.	**mustaHDar liTard 'alHasharaat**
	مستحضر لطرد الحشرات .
—some sanitary towels.	**manaashif SiHHiyyah**
	مناشف صحیّة .
—some Tampax.	**tampaks**
	تامبكس .
—some paper tissue.	**maHaarim (manaadeel) waraq**
	محارم (منادیل) ورق .
*What is wrong with you?	**ma bik/biky**
	ما بك ؟

(see section on 'Medical Treatment' for describing symptoms).

Can you prepare this prescription, please?	**mumkin tuHaDDir/tuHaDDiry** **haadhih 'alwaSfah min faDlak/** **faDlik**
	ممکن تحضر هذه الوصفة من فضلك ؟

Cosmetic Items

Please can I have ...	min faDlak/faDlik 'a9Teeny
	من فضلك أعطيني . . . .
–some soap.	Saaboon
	صابون .
–some toothpaste.	ma9joon 'asnaan
	معجون أسنان .
–some shampoo.	shampoo
	شامبو .
–some deodorant.	muzeel liraa'iHat 'al9araq
	مزيل لرائحة العرق .
–some make-up.	mustaHDaraat tajmeel
	مستحضرات تجميل .
–some suntan lotion.	looshin Didd 'ashshams
	لوشن ضد الشمس .
–some face cream.	kreem lilwajh
	كريم للوجه .
–some lip cream.	kreem lishshifaah
	كريم للشفاه .
–some body lotion.	looshin liljism
	لوشن للجسم .
–some hand cream.	kreem lilyadayn
	كريم لليدين .

−some razor blades.	shafraat Hilaaqah
	شفرات حلاقة .
−some shaving cream.	kreem Hilaaqah
	كريم حلاقة .
−some shaving soap.	Saaboon Hilaaqah
	صابون حلاقة .
−some after-shave.	looshin ba9d 'alHilaaqah
	لوشن بعد الحلاقة .
−a razor.	maakeenat Hilaaqah
	ماكينه حلاقه .

GENERAL NOTICES

	الوصفات الطبية .
Prescriptions	'alwaSfaat 'aTTubiyyah
	سمّ
Poison	summ
	للاستعمال الخارجي فقط .
For external use only	lil'isti9maal 'alkhaarijy faqaT
	تعليمات للإستعمال
Directions for use	ta9leemaat lil'isti9maal

Clothes and accessories

*Can I help you?	**mumkin 'asaa9dak/'asaa9dik**
	ممكن أساعدك ؟
No, I'm just looking, thank you.	**laa, 'anaa 'atafarraj faqaT, shukran**
	لا ، أنا أتفرّج فقط ، شكرا .
I'd like ...	**'ureed**
	أريد . . . .
–a coat (long).	**mi9Taf (Taweel)**
	معطف (طويل)
–a jacket (short).	**jakayt/sutrah (qaSeerah)**
	جاكيت / سترة (قصيرة)
–a cardigan (medium-length).	**jakayt Soof ('aTTool wasaT)**
	جاكيت صوف (الطول وسط)
–a dress (day).	**fustaan (linnahaar)**
	فستان (للنهار)
–(evening)	**(lissahrah)**
	(للسهرة)

(See Reference Section for colours)

*What size are you?	**ma qiyaasak/qiyaasik**
	ما قياسك ؟
I'm size	**qiyaasy**
	قياسي . . . .

(Sizes of clothes available in shops in the Arab countries depend on the country of origin. Locally made clothes are usually in English or French sizes. Shopkeepers can be of help in assessing your size and it is always advisable to try on clothes before buying them.)

It's too ...	**huwa ... jiddan**
	هو . . . جدًا
–tight.	**Dayyiq**
	ضيّق
–long.	**Taweel**
	طويل
–thick.	**sameek**
	سميك
–loose.	**waasi9**
	واسع
–short.	**qaSeer**
	قصير
–big.	**kabeer**
	كبير
–thin (light).	**raqeeq (khafeef)**
	رقيق (خفيف)
It doesn't suit me.	**laa yunaasibny**
	لا يناسبني
It doesn't fit me.	**lays 9alaa qiyaasy**
	ليس على قياسي

Have you got it in	9indakum mithluh bilawn
	عندكم مثله بلون ....
–red?	'aHmar
	أحمر ؟
–brown?	bunny
	بني ؟
–green?	'akhDar
	أخضر ؟
–blue?	'azraq
	أزرق ؟
Do you keep ...?	hal tabee9oon
	هل تبيعون .... ؟
Can you show me ...?	mumkin 'araa
	ممكن أرى .... ؟
–skirts?	tanaaneer (joonillaat)
	تنانير (جونلات) ؟
–underwear?	thiyaab daakhiliyyah
	ثياب داخلية ؟
–blouses?	bloozaat
	بلوزات ؟
–nightwear?	qumSaan nawm
	قمصان نوم ؟
This is just what I wanted.	hadhaa maa 'ureed biZZabT
	هذا ما أريد بالظبط .

How much is it?	**kam si9ruh** كم سعره ؟
Do you take credit cards?	**hal ta'khudhoon biTaaqaat kradit** هل تأخذون بطاقات كرديت ؟
Please, may I have a receipt?	**min faDlak/faDlik 'a9Teeny waSl** من فضلك أعطيني وصل ؟
I'd like to change this.	**'ureed tabdeel haadhaa** أريد تبديل هذا .
I bought it two days ago.	**'ishtaraytuh min yawmayn** إشتريتة من يومين .
–one week ago.	**min 'usboo9** من أسبوع
Where can I buy ...?	**'ayn 'aqdar 'ashtary** أين أقدر أشتري . . . . . ؟

Shoes

I'd like a pair of ...	**'ureed zawj** أريد زوج . . . .
–walking shoes.	**Hidhaa' lilmashy** حذاء للمشي
–smart shoes.	**Hidhaa' 'aneeq (rasmy)** حذاء أنيق (رسمي)

–beach shoes.	**Hidhaa' lishshaaTi'** حذاء للشاطئ
–beach sandals.	**Sandal lishshaaTi'** صندل للشاطئ .
–sandals.	**Sandal** صندل
–tennis shoes.	**Hidhaa' riyaaDah** حذاء رياضة
–boots.	**jazmah** جزمة
I'm afraid I don't like …	**lil'asaf laa 'uHibb** للأسف لا أحب . . . .
–the style.	**'almooDah** الموضة
–the colour.	**'allawn** اللون
The heels are too high.	**'alka9b 9aaly jiddan** الكعب عالي جدًا
–too low.	**waaTy jiddan** واطي جدًا
They're too small.	**heeya Sagheerah jiddan** هي صغيرة جدًا
–too big.	**kabeerah jiddan** كبيرة جدًا

VOCABULARY

socks	kalsaat (jawaairb) qaSeerah	كلسات (جوارب) قصيرة
underpants (ladies')	libaas (keelutt)	لباس (كيلوت)
(men's)	kalsoon	كلسون
stockings	kalsaat (jawaarib) Taweelah	كلسات (جوارب) طويلة
tights	kullaan	كولان
bra	Sadriyyah (sootyaan)	صدريه (سوتيان)
petticoat	tannoorah taHtaaniyyah (shalHah)	تنورة تحتانية (شلحة)
vest	Sadriyyah rijjaaliyyah	صدرية رجاليه
shirt	qameeS	قميص
blouse	bloozah	بلوزة
cardigan	jaakayt Soof	جاكيت صوف
pullover	kanzah	كنزه
jacket	jaakayt (sutrah)	جاكبت (سترة)
skirt	tannoorah (joonillah)	تنورة (جونله)

trousers (ladies' and men's)	banTaloon	بنطلون
trouser suit	Taqm (banTaloon ma9 jaakayt)	طقم (بنطلون مع جاكيت)
suit (ladies')	Taqm	طقم
(men's)	Taqm (badhlah rijjaaly)	طقم (بذله رجالي)
tie	rabTat 9unq (kraavaat)	ربطة عنق (كرافات)
dress	fustaan	فستان .
long dress	fustaan Taweel	فستان طويل .
scarf	'iysharp	إيشارب .
hat	burnayTah (qubba9ah)	برنيطه (قبعه) .
cap	Taaqiyyah	طاقيّة .
raincoat	mi9Taf lilmaTar	معطف للمطر
coat	mi9Taf (kabboot)	معطف (كبوت)
umbrella	shamsiyyah	شمسيه
bikini	bikeeny (mayyuh qiT9atayn)	بيكيني (مايوه قطعتين)
swimming costume	mayyuh (thawb sibaaHah)	مايوه (ثوب سباحة)

swimming trunks	mayyuh rijjaaly	مايوه رجالى
tee-shirt	qameeS quTn	قميص قطن
shorts	banTaloon qaSeer	بنطلون قصير

Some Common Materials

What's it made of?	maa naw9 haadhaa 'alqimaash	مانوع هذا القماش ؟
I'd like it in	'ureeduh min	أريده من . . . .
wool	Soof	صوف
cotton	quTn	قطن
nylon	naylun	نايلون
acrylic	naseej Sinaa9y	نسيج صناعى
fur	faroo	فرو
leather	jild	جلد
suede	jild mukhmaly (shamwaa)	جلد مخملى (شاموا)
silk	Hareer	حرير
corduroy	mukhmal muDalla9	مخمل مضلّع
velvet	mukhmal	مخمل
jersey (cotton)	jirsay (quTny)	جيرسيه (قطني)
(wool)	(Soofy)	(صوفي)
linen	kittaan	كتان

Photography

I'd like ... please.	'ureed ... min faDlak/faDlik
	أريد . . . . من فضلك .
–a film for this camera	film li'aalat 'attaSweer haadhih
	فيلم لآلة التصوير هذه .
–a black and white film	film 'abyaD wa 'aswad
	فيلم أبيض وأسود .
–a colour print film	film Soowar mulawwan
	فيلم صور ملون .
–a colour slide film	film slayds mulawwan
	فيلم سلايدزملوّن .
–an 8-mm film	film thamaaniyat millymitr
	فيلم ثمانية ميليمتر .
–a 35-mm film	film khamsat wa thalaatheen millymitr
	فيلم ٣٥ ميليمتر .
–some flash bulbs	lambaat lilflash
	لمبات للفلاش .
With twenty exposures	bi9ishreen Soorah
	بعشرين صورة .
With thirty-six exposures	bisittat wa thalaatheen Soorah
	بسته وثلاثين صورة .
Do you print photos?	hal taTba9oon Soowar
	هل تطبعون صور ؟

How much does it cost?	kam yukallif
	كم يكلف ؟
Is developing included?	hal 'attaZheer maHsoob
	هل التظهير محسوب ؟
I'd like this film developed.	'ureed taZheer haadhaa 'alfilm
	أريد تظهير هذا الفيلم .
–printed.	Tab9
	طبع .
I'd like this photo enlarged.	'ureed takbeer haadhih 'aSSoorah
	أريد تكبير هذه الصور .
With a glossy/matt finish.	9alaa waraq lammaa9/ghayr maSqool
	على ورق لمّاع / غير مصقول .
I'd like (four) prints of this one.	'ureed ('arba9) nusakh min haadhih
	أريد (أربع) نسخ من هذه .
When will it be ready?	mataa takoon jaahizah
	متى تكون جاهزة ؟
When will they be ready?	mataa yakoonoon jaahizeen
	متى يكونون جاهزين ؟
Please can you mend my camera?	min faDlak/faDlik mumkin tuSalliH/tuSalliHy 'aalat 'attaSweer
	من فضلك ممكن تصلّح آله التصوير ؟

Please can you take out the film?	**min faDlak/faDlik mumkin tasHab/tasHaby 'alfilm**

من فصلك ممكن تسحب الفيلم ؟

The film is stuck.	**'alfilm mashbook**

الفيلم مشبوك .

Books and stationery

Do you keep English newspapers?	**hal tabee9oon jaraayid 'ingleeziyyah**

هل تبيعون جرايد إنجليزية ؟

Do you have English books?	**9indakum kutub 'ingleeziyyah**

عندكم كتب إنجليزية ؟

Do you sell road maps?	**hal tabee9oon kharaa'iT liTTuruq**

هل تبيعون خرائط للطرق ؟

I'd like	**'ureed**

أريد . . . .

–a map.	**khaariTah**

خارطه .

–a guide-book.	**daleel siyaaHy**

دليل سياحى .

–a post-card.	**biTaaqah bareediyyah**

بطاقه بريديّه .

–a notebook.	**daftar mulaaHaZaat**
	دفتر ملاحظات .
–an exercise book.	**daftar**
	دفتر .
–a pen.	**qalam Hibr**
	قلم حبر .
–a biro.	**qalam Hibr naashif**
	قلم حبر ناشف .
–a pencil.	**qalam raSaaS**
	قلم رصاص .
–a rubber.	**maHHaayah**
	محايّه .
–some writing-paper.	**waraq lilkitaabah**
	ورق للكتابه .
–some ink.	**Hibr**
	حبر
–some envelopes.	**mughallafaat (Zuroof)**
	مغلّفات (ظروف)
–some sellotape.	**shareeT laaSiq (skutsh tayp)**
	شريط لاصق (سكوتش تايب) .
–some string.	**khayT**
	خيط .
–some brown paper.	**waraq bunnee**
	ورق بني .

–some tie-on labels.

biTaaqaat tamreek ma9 ribaaT

بطاقات تمريك مع رباط .

–some stick-on labels.

biTaaqaat tamreek laaSiqah

بطاقات تمريك لاصقه .

Restaurants, Cafés and Bars

Reserving a Table

Can you recommend a
good restaurant?

mumkin tanSaHny/tanSaHeeny
bimaT9am jayyid

ممكن تنصحني بمطعم جيد ؟

I'd like to book a table.

'ureed 'an 'aHjiz Taawilah

أريد أن أحجز طاوله .

For four people.

li'arba9 'ashkhaaS

لأربع أشخاص .

At eight o'clock.

lissaa9ah thamaaniyah

للساعة ثمانيه .

*I'm sorry, we're all
booked up tonight.

'aasif/'aasifah kul
'aTTaawilaat 'maHajoozah
haadhih 'allaylah

آسف كل الطاولات محجوزه هذه
الليلة .

I've reserved a table.

'anaa Hajazt Taawilah

أنا حجزت طاوله .

My name is ....

'ismy

إسمى . . . .

Have you a table for two?

9indakum Taawilah lishakhSayn

عندكم طاولة لشخصين ؟

We're in a hurry.

naHn musta9jiloon

نحن مستعجلون .

Ordering Your Meal
(See the following section for an example of a typical menu)

Can we see the menu,
please?

mumkin naraa qaa'imat
'aTTa9aam min faDlak/faDlik

ممكن نرى قائمه الطعام من
فضلك ؟

Can I have the wine-list?

mumkin ta9Teeny qaa'imat
'almashroobaat

ممكن تعطيني قائمة المشروبات ؟

What's this?

maa haadhaa

ما هذا ؟

What do you recommend?	bimaadhaa tanSaHnaa/ tanSaHeenaa

بماذا تنصحنا ؟

Are vegetables included?	hal haadhaa yashmal 'alkhuDrawaat

هل هذا يشمل الخضروات ؟

Is the drink included?	hal haadhaa yashmal 'almashroob

هل هذا يشمل المشروب ؟

I'll have	s'aakhudh

سآخذ . . . . .

*How do you like your steak done?	kayf tureed/tureedy 'asstayk

كيف تريد الستيك ؟

Rare.	ghayr mustawy

غير مستوي

Medium rare.	wasaT

وسط

Well done.	mustawy jayyidan

مستوي جيدا

Do you sell wine by the glass?	hal tabee9oon ka's nabeedh faqaT

هل تبيعون كأس نبيذ فقط ؟

We'd like ...	nureed

نريد . . . . .

– a bottle of local wine.

qanneenat nabeedh maHally

قنينه نبيذ محلى .

– a carafe of local wine.

dawraq nabeedh maHally

دورق نبيذ محلى .

– some red wine.

nabeedh 'aHmar

نبيذ أحمر

– some white wine.

nabeedh 'abyaD

نبيذ أبيض

– some rosé.

nabeedh ruzay

نبيذ روزاي

– a glass of beer.

ka's beerah

كأس بيره

– some water.

maa'

ماء

Could I have some more
...?

mumkin 'aakhudh ziyaadah

ممكن آخذ زياده . . . . ؟

Complaints and Questions
This isn't what I ordered.

haadhaa ghayr maa Talabt

هذا غير ما طلبت

There's a mistake.

hunaak khaTa'

هناك خطأ

This is dirty.

haadhaa wasikh

هذا وسخ .

– cold.

baarid

بارد .

– stale.

ghayr Taazij

غير طازج .

Please change the ....

min faDlak ghayyir/faDlik ghayyiry haadhaa

من فضلك غيّر هذا . . . .

The fish is bad.

'assammak 9aaTil

السمك عاطل .

– not cooked.

ghayr mustawy

. . غير مستوى .

I'd like to see the manager.

'ureed 'an 'araa 'almudeer

أريد أن أرى المدير .

*We've run out of ....

khalaS min 9indnaa

خلص من عندنا . . . .

Where's the lavatory?

'ayn 'almirHaad

أين المرحاض ؟

Paying the Bill

Can I have the bill, please?

mumkin ta9Teeny 'alfaatoorah min faDlak/faDlik

ممكن تعطيني الفاتوره من فضلك ؟

What is this charge for?

limaadhaa haadhih 'al'ujrah

لماذا هذه الأجرة ؟

I think there's a mistake.	**'aZunn hunaak khaTa'**
	أظن هناك خطأ .
I didn't have	**lam 'aakhudh**
	لم آخذ . . . .
I didn't order	**lam 'aTlub**
	لم أطلب . . . .
Is service included?	**hal 'alkhidmah maHsoobah**
	هل الخدمه محسوبه ؟
Thank you very much.	**shukran jazeelan**
	شكرا جزيلا .
It was a very good meal.	**kaanat wajbah mumtaazah**
	كانت وجبه ممتازة .
Goodbye.	**ma9 'assalaamah**
	مع السلامة

Food in the Arab world

In the Levant (Lebanon, Syria and Jordan) the cuisine is mediter-
ranean in nature.

Lebanon is a gourmet's paradise. The world famous Lebanese
Mezze comprises some sixty odd dishes served as hors-d'oeuvre
with the local aniseed flavoured drink '**Arak**'. It is a feast for the
eyes and the palate! The main course (if you can find room for it)
is again a variety of charcoal grilled meats, birds, kibbih etc. ...

In the Gulf you can enjoy, in addition to the huge prawns and
very tasty fish (**Haamoor**), a whole lamb on a mountain of rice! In
most of the Gulf states liquor is prohibited.

Arabic bread comes in many varieties ranging from paper-thin sheets baked on wood fires to round, slightly leavened double-layered bakers' loaves.

Turkish coffee is a boiled suspension of finely ground coffee, water, sugar and sometimes, cardamom. When ordering Turkish coffee, specify the amount of sugar you require:

very sweet	**sukkar katheer**	سكر كثير
medium	**maDbooTah (wasaT)**	مضبوطة (وسط)
little sugar	**sukkar qaleel**	سكر قليل
without sugar	**bidoon sukkar**	بدون سكر

Bedouin coffee is weak, without sugar and strongly flavoured with cardamom, It is served as a sign of hospitality in very small amounts, in tiny cups. Tradition imposes that you take a minimum of three cups after which you can shake your cup to indicate that you've had enough.

Smoking a hubble bubble (**narjeelah**) after a large meal can be a pleasant experience.

While in the old sooks in Damascus, try the pounded pistachio ice-cream.

SOME ARABIC DISHES

Hors-d'Oeuvre

فول مدمّس

Baked beans salad with a vinaig-   **fool mudammas**
rette dressing

حمّص بطحينه

Chick peas in sesame oil sauce   **HummuS biTaHeenah**

فلافل

Small fried bean balls	**falaafil**

تبّوله

Parsley salad	**tabboolih**

باذنجان متبّل

Grilled aubergines in sesame oil sauce	**batinjaan mutabbal**

محدّره

Esau's dish of lentils	**mujaddarah**

سمبوسك

Pastries with meat and pine kernels	**samboosik**

فطاير بسبانخ

Spinach turnovers	**faTaayir bisabaanikh**

عجّة

Omelet	**9ijjah**

كما

Desert truffles	**kamaa (fagr)**

Main Dishes

كبّه

Meat pounded with cracked wheat (grilled, fried, baked or cooked in yoghurt)	**kibbih**

Alternating layers of meat and fat grilled on an upright spit	شاورما **shawarmaa**
Meat loaf grilled on skewers	كباب **kabaab**
Stuffed baby lamb	قوزى **qoozy**
Couscous	مغربيّة **mughrabiyyah**
Fish and rice	صياديّه **Sayyaadiyyah**
Type of baby pizza with meat and pine kernels	صفيحه **SfeeHah**
Stew of a leafy vegetable served with rice, chicken, croutes and onions in lemon	ملوخيّه **mulookhiyyah**
Stuffed vine leaves	ورق عنب **waraq 9inab**
Layered dish of meat, rice, bread soaked in stock and yoghurt with garlic	فتّه **fattih**

Desserts

Multi-layered pastries	بقلاوه **baqlaawah**
Small baqlaawah	كل واشكر **kul washkur**
Pastry covered with sesame seeds and syrup	برازق **baraaziq**
Shredded wheat over goat cheese baked in sugar syrup	كنافه **kinaafah**
Semolina pastry cakes filled with nuts	معمول **ma9mool**
Blanc-mange	مهلّبيّه **muhallabiyyah**
Ice cream	بوظه **booZah**

VOCABULARY

ashtray	**manfaDah**	منفضه
glass	**kubbaayah**	كبايه
knife	**sikkeen**	سكين
fork	**shawkah**	شوكه
spoon	**mil9aqah**	ملعقه

teaspoon	mil9aqat shaay	ملعقة شاى
cup	finjaan	فنجان
plate	SaHn	صحن
napkin	fooTat sufrah	فوطه سفره
salt	milH	ملح
pepper	filfil	فلفل
mustard	khardal	خردل
salad dressing	tawaabil 'assalaTah	توابل السلطه
sauce	SalSah	صلصه
tea	shaay	شاى
coffee	qahwah	قهوة
mineral water	maa' ma9daniyyah	ماء معدنيه
milk	Haleeb	حليب
brandy	kunyaak	كونياك
sherry	shary	شرى
lemonade	limunaaDah	يموناضه
orange squash	9aSeer burtuqaal	عصير برتقال
fruit juice	9aSeer faakihah	عصير فاكهه
fizzy	fawwaar	فوّار
still	ghayr fawwaar	غير فوّار
raw	nay' (ghayr maTbookh)	نىء

(See the section 'In a food shop' for the names of meats, fruits, etc.)

Methods of Cooking
These words will appear on the menu as descriptions of the way the meat or fish has been cooked:

smoked	**mudakhkhan**
	مدخّن
baked	**makhbooz bilfurn**
	مخبوز بالفرن
fried	**maqly**
	مقلى
braised	**musabbak**
	مسبّك
boiled	**maslooq**
	مسلوق
stuffed	**maHshy**
	محشي
roast	**muHammar**
	محمّر
grilled	**mashwy**
	مشوى

At the Hairdresser or Barber

I'd like to make an appointment for ...	'ureed 'an 'aakhudh maw9id li أريد أن آخذ موعد لـ . . . .
I'd like my hair ... -	'ureed ... sha9ry أريد . . . شعرى
–cut.	qaSS قص .
–washed.	ghaseel غسيل .
–trimmed.	qaS 'aTraaf قصّ أطراف

—set.	**taSfeef**
	تصفيف .
—re-styled.	**taghyeer taSfeef**
	تغيير تصفيف .
—permed.	**taj9eed**
	تجعيد .
—straightened.	**tamlees**
	تمليس .
—tinted.	**Sabgh khafeef**
	صبغ خفيف .
—dyed.	**Sabgh**
	صبغ .
—blow-dried.	**tansheef bilfard**
	تنشيف بالفرد .
*How much do you want cut?	**kam tureed/tureedy 'an 'aquSS**
	كم تريد أن أقصّ ؟
Not much.	**lays katheer**
	ليس كثير .
A lot.	**katheer**
	كثير .
Not too short.	**lays qaSeer jiddan**
	ليس قصير جدا .

Not very short on top.   lays qaSeer min 'al'a9laa

ليس قصير من الأعلى .

−at the sides.   9alaa 'aljaanibayn

على الجانبين .

That's enough.   haadhaa kaafy

هذا كافي .

Please cut more off the back.   min faDlak quSS/faDlik quSSy 'akthar min 'alkhalf

من فضلك قصّ أكثر من الخلف .

−the sides.   'aljaanibayn

الجانبين .

−the top   'al'a9laa

الأعلى .

I'm in a hurry.   'anaa musta9jil/musta9jilah

أنا مستعجل .

The drier is too hot.   'almunashshif Haar jiddan

المنشف حارجدا .

−too cold.   baarid jiddan

بارد جدا .

I'd like ...   'ureed

أريد . . . .

−a shave.   Hilaaqat dhaqny

حلاقه ذقني .

–a manicure.	**taqleem 'aZaafiry**
	تقليم أظافرى .
–some nail-polish.	**Tilaa 'aZaafir**
	طلاء أظافر .
–some setting lotion.	**looshin littaSfeef**
	لوشن للتصفيف
–some conditioner.	**condishinar**
	كوند يشنار

Laundry/Dry-cleaning

Please can you clean ...   **min faDlak/faDlik mumkin tanZeef**

من فضلك ممكن تنظيف . . . .

–these clothes.   **haadhih 'aththiyaab**

هذه الثياب .

–this coat.   **haadhaa 'almi9Taf**

هذا المعطف .

–this raincoat.   **mi9Taf 'almaTar haadhaa**

معطف المطر هذا .

–this skirt.   **haadhih 'attannoorah**

هذه التنوره .

–this jacket.   **haadhih 'aljaakayt**

هذه الجاكيت .

–these trousers.

haadhaa 'albanTaloon

هذا البنطلون .

I'd like ... washed.

'ureed ghaseel

أريد غسيل . . . .

Please can you remove
this stain?

min faDlak/faDlik mumkin
'izaalat haadhih 'albuq9ah

من فضلك ممكن إزالة هذه
البقعه ؟

Please re-proof.

min faDlak/faDlik tajdeed man9
'annashsh fee haadhaa
'alqimaash

من فضلك تجديد منع النشّ في
هذا القماش .

–mend

taSleeH

تصليح

–press

kawy

كوى

Can you launder these
shirts, please?

mumkin ghaseel wa kawy
haadhih 'alqumSaan min faDlak/
faDlik

ممكن غسيل وكوى هذه القمصان
من فضلك ؟

I need it as soon as
possible.

'aHtaajuhaa fee 'aqrab waqt
mumkin

أحتاجها في أقرب وقت ممكن .

Can you do it express?

mumkin 9amalhaa bisur9ah
faa'iqah

ممكن عملها بسرعة فائقه ؟

When will it be ready?

mataa takoon jahizah

متى تكون جاهزه ؟

This is still dirty.

haadhaa maa zaal wasikh

هذا ما زال وسخ .

I don't want to pay.

laa 'ureed 'an 'adfa9

لا أريد أن أدفع .

At the Bank

Please change this into . . .

**min faDlak 'uSruf/faDlik
'uSrufy haadhaa 'ilaa**

من فضلك أصرف هذا إلى . . . .

Please cash these cheques.

**min faDlak 'uSruf/faDlik
'uSrufy haadhih 'ashshikaat**

من فضلك أصرف هـذه
الشيكات .

Can I have it in notes,
please?

**mumkin 'aakhudhhaa bi'awraaq
naqdiyyah minfaDlak/faDlik**

ممكن آخذها بأوراق نقديه من
فضلك ؟

Can I have it in small change, please?

mumkin 'aakhudhhaa firaaTah (fakkah) min faDlak/faDlik

ممكن آخذها فراطه (فكّه) من فضلك ؟

Has my bank transfer arrived?

hal waSalat Hiwaalaty 'almaSrafiyyah

هل وصلت حوالتي المصرفيه ؟

Can you cable my bank?

mumkin 'irsaal barqiyyah 'ilaa maSrafy

ممكن إرسال برقيه إلى مصرفي ؟

How long will it take?

kam ta'khudh min 'alwaqt

كم تأخذ من الوقت ؟

*Up to a week.

'aqSaa Hadd 'usboo9

أقصى حد أسبوع .

(See 'Reference Section' for numbers and dates)

At the Post Office

How much is a letter for England?	**kam 'ujrat 'arrisaalah 'ilaa 'inglitarraa**
	كم أجرة الرساله إلى إنجلترا ؟
How much is a postcard to England?	**kam 'ujrat biTaaqah bareediyyah 'ilaa 'inglitarraa**
	كم أجرة بطاقه بريديه إلى إنجلترا ؟

(See 'Reference Section' for other countries)

Please give me . . .	**min faDlak/faDlik 'a9Teeny**
	من فضلك أعطيني . . . .
–a . . . stamp.	**Taaba9 bareed bi**
	طابع بريد بـ . . . . .
–an aerogram.	**'istimaarah jawwiyyah**
	إسماره جويّه .

–a telegram form.	'istimaarah barqiyyah
	إستماره برقيه .
I want to send .... to ...	'ureed 'irsaal ... 'ilaa
	أريد إرسال . . . إلى .
–a telegram.	barqiyyah
	برقيّه .
–a parcel.	ruzmah
	رزمه .
–an international money order.	Hiwaalah maaliyyah dawliyyah
	حواله ماليّه دوليّه .
How much is it per word?	kam 'ujrat 'alkalimah
	كم أجرة الكلمه ؟
Reply paid.	'aljawaab madfoo9 'al'ujrah
	الجواب مدفوع الأجره .
Can I have a customs declaration form?	mumkin 'aakhudh'istimaarat taSreeH (bayaan) jumruky
	ممكن آخذ إستماره تصريح (بيان) جمركى ؟
I'd like to send this	'ureed 'irsaal haadhaa
	أريد إرسال هذا . . . .
–surface mail.	bareed 9aady
	بريد عادى .
–air mail.	bareed jawwy
	بريد جوّى .

–registered.	musajjal
	. مسجّل
–express.	musta9jal
	. مستعجل
–recorded delivery.	ma9 waSl bil'istilaam
	. مع وصل بالاستلام

WRITTEN POSTAL INSTRUCTIONS

Do not bend	laa taTwy
	. لا تطو
Fragile	qaabil lilkasr
	. قابل للكسر
Urgent	musta9jal
	. مستعجل

Poste restante

Where's the Poste Restante counter?	'ayn shubbaak tawzee9 'arrassaa'il
	أين شبّاك توزيع الرسائل ؟
Is there any post for me?	hal min rasaa'il lee
	هل من رسائل لى ؟
*What's your name?	maa 'ismak/ismik
	ما اسمك ؟
My name is ...	'Ismy
	اسمى . . . .

Have you got your passport?	**9indak/9indik jawaaz safarak/safarik** عندك جواز سفرك ؟
When's the next delivery?	**mataa maw9id 'attawzee9 'attaaly** متى موعد التوزيع التالى ؟
When's the last delivery today?	**mataa 'aakhir tawzee9 'alyawm** متى آخر توزيع اليوم ؟
Could you please forward my mail?	**mumkin taHweel rasaa'ily** ممكن تحويل رسائلى ؟
Here's my forwarding address.	**haadhaa 9unwaany 'alqaadim** هذا عنوانى القادم .

Telephoning

Is there a phone here?	**hal yoojad talifoon hunaa**
	هل يوجد تلفون هنا ؟
Please may I use the phone?	**min faDlak/faDlik tismaHly 'asta9mil attalifoon**
	من فضلك تسمحلى أستعمل التلفون ؟
Where's the nearest phone-box?	**'ayn 'aqrab talifoon 9umoomy**
	أين أقرب تلفون عمومى ؟

Direct dialling

Hello, this is ...	**hello 'anaa**
	هلو أنا . . . .

Can I speak to …, please.	mumkin 'atakallam ma9 … min faDlak/faDlik
	ممكن أتكلم مع . . . من فضلك ؟
Hold on, please.	'intaZir, laa tatruk/tatruky 'al-khatt min faDlak/faDlik
	انتظر ، لا تترك الخط من فضلك .
Extension … please.	far9 … min faDlak/faDlik
	فرع . . . من فضلك .
Can I leave a message, please?	mumkin 'atruk risaalah min faDlak/faDlik
	ممكن أترك رسالة من فضلك ؟
Sorry, I've got the wrong number.	'aasif 'arraqm khaTa'
	آسف ، الرقم خطأ .
*I'll call you back.	'attaSil feek/feeky ba9dayn
	أتصل فيك بعدين .
*There's no reply.	ma fee jawaab
	ما في جواب .
I'll try again later.	sa'uHaawil marrah thaaniah ba9dayn
	سأحاول مرة ثانية بعدين .
*Who's speaking?	man yatakallam
	من يتكلم ؟
Goodbye.	ma9 assalaamah
	مع السلامه .

Calls made via the operator

I'd like to make a personal
call to ...

**'ureed tasjeel mukhaabarah
shakhSiyyah 'ila**

أريد تسجيل مخابره شخصيه
إلى . . . .

I'd like to make a reverse
charge call to

**'ureed tasjeel mukhaabarah
yadfa9 'aTTaraf 'al'aakhar
'ujratahaa 'ila**

أريد تسجيل مخابرة يدفع الطرف
الآخر أجرتها إلى . . . .

What's your number?

maa raqmak

ما رقمك ؟

I'd like to make a call to
England.

**'ureed tasjeel mukhaabarah
'ila 'ingliterra**

أريد تسجيل مخابره إلى إنجلترا .

Can I book a call for ...
o'clock?

**mumkin 'aHjiz mukhaabarah
lissaa 9ah**

ممكن أحجز مخابره للساعه . . . . ؟

What's the delay?
(i.e. how long?)

kam tata'akhkhar

كم تتأخر ؟

How much will it cost?

kam tukallif

كم تكلّف ؟

For ... minutes.

li daqaa'iq

لـ . . . دقائق .

*The line's engaged.

'alkhaTT mashghool

الخط مشغول .

*Replace the receiver.

sakkir/sakkiry 'assammaa9ah

سكّر السمّاعه .

*Don't replace the
receiver.

laa tusakkir/tusakkiry
assammaa9ah

لا تسكّر السمّاعه .

I've been cut off.

'inqaTa9 'alkhatt

إنقطع الخط .

Please could you
reconnect me?

min faDlak/faDlik mumkin
tooSilny marrah thaniyah

من فضلك ممكن توصلني مرّه
ثانيه ؟

The phone's out of
order

attalifoon mu 9aTTal

التلفون معطّل .

Medical Treatment

For the doctor

Where's the nearest
doctor?

'ayn 'aqrab Tabeeb

أين أقرب طبيب ؟

Must I make an
appointment?

yajib 'an 'aakhudh maw9id

يجب أن آخذ موعد ؟

Does he speak English?

hal yatakallam 'ingleezy

هل يتكلم إنجليزى ؟

It's an emergency.

Haalat Tawaari'

حاله طوارىء .

Ring for an ambulance.

'ittaSil bil'is9aaf

إتّصل بالإسعاف .

Most frequent complaints

My ... aches	**yu'limuny** يؤلمني . . . .
–stomach	**ma9idaty tu'limuny** معدتي تؤلمني
–chest	**Sadry yu'limuny** صدري يؤلمني
–ear	**'udhuny tu'limuny** أذني تؤلمني
head	**ra'sy yu'limuny** رأسي يؤلمني
–back	**Zahry yu'limuny** ظهري يؤلمني
I've got a temperature.	**9indy Haraarah** عندي حراره
I've got a ...	**9indy** عندي . . . .
–cough.	**Sa9lah (qaHHah)** سعلة (قحّه) .
–cold.	**rashaH** رشح .
–sore throat.	**bal9oom multahib** بلعوم ملتهب .

–migraine.	Sudaa9 (waja9 ra's)
	صداع (وجع رأس) .
–stiff neck.	raqbah mutaSallibah
	رقبة متصلّبة .
–rash.	TafH
	طفح .
I've got....	9indy
	عندى ....
–constipation.	'imsaak
	إمساك .
–indigestion.	9usr haDn
	عسر هضم .
–cramp.	tashannuj 9aDalaat
	تشنّج عضلات .
–sunstroke.	Darbat shams
	ضربة شمس .
I feel....	'ash9ur
	أشعر ....
–dizzy.	bidawkhah
	بدوخة .
–faint.	9alaa washak 'al'ighmaa'
	على وشك الإغماء .
–sick.	9alaa washak 'attaqayu'
	على وشك التقيّؤ .

I can't ....

laa 'aqdar 'an...

لا أقدر أن . . . .

–sleep.

'anaam

أنام .

–breathe.

'atanaffas

أتنفّس .

–eat anything.

'aakul shay'

آكل شيء .

–pass water.

'atabawwal

أتبوّل .

I think I've got ...

'aZunn 9indy ...

أظن عندى . . . .

–food poisoning.

tasammum 'akl

تسمم أكل

–urinary infection.

'iltihaab bawly

إلتهاب بولى .

–sinusitis.

'iltihaab 'aljuyoob 'al'anfiyyah

إلتهاب الجيوب الأنفيّه .

I've twisted my ....

lawayt

لويت . . . .

–wrist.

mi9Samy

معصمى .

–arm.

dhiraa9y

ذراعى .

–leg.	saaqy
	ساقي .
–ankle	kaaHily
	كاحلي .
–back.	Zahry
	ظهري .
*Where does it hurt?	'ayn 'al'alm
	أين الألم ؟
*Tell me when it hurts.	qul/qooly lee 9indamaa tata'allam/tata'allamy
	قل لي عندما تتألم .
*How long has it been like this?	mundh mataa 'alHaalah haakadhaa
	منذ متى الحالة هكذا ؟

Personal details and requests

Can I have a prescription for … ?	mumkin 'aakhudh waSfah li'ajl
	ممكن آخذ وصفه لأجل . . . ؟
Can you inoculate me against … ?	mumkin tulaqqiHny/ tulaqqiHeeny Didd
	ممكن تلقّحني ضد . . . ؟
I'm on the pill.	'aakhudh Huboob man9 'alHaml
	آخذ حبوب منع الحمل .

I take pills for...	'aakhudh Huboob li'ajl
	آخذ حبوب لأجل ....
I've lost my...	Dayya9t
	ضيّعت ....
–pills.	Hubooby
	حبوبي .
–prescription	waSfaty
	وصفتي .
–glasses.	naZZaaraaty
	نظّاراتي .
I'm allergic to...	9indy Hasaasiyyah li
	عندي حساسيّة لـ ....
I'm pregnant.	'anaa Haamil
	أنا حامل
I'm a diabetic.	9indy sukkary
	عندي سكّري
I'm asthmatic.	9indy raboo
	عندى ربو .
I'm an epileptic.	9indy daa' 'aSSara9
	عندى داء الصرع .
I have a heart condition.	9indy Haalah maraDiyyah fee 'alqalb
	عندى حالة مرضيّة في القلب .

I'm worried about my
baby.

baaly mashghool 9alaa Tifly

بالى مشغول على طفلى .

He won't eat.

yarfuD 'al'akl

يرفض الأكل .

He can't swallow.

laa yaqdir 'an yabla9

لا يقدر أن يبلع .

At the dentist's

My tooth aches
(very badly).

sinny yu'limuny (jiddan)

سنّى يؤلمنى (جدا) .

A filling has come out.

Hashwat Dirsy Tala9at

حشوه ضرسي طلعت .

– broken.

maksoorah

مكسوره .

My tooth has broken.

sinny 'inkasar

سنّى إنكسر .

My gums are very sore.

laththaty multahibah

لثتي ملتهبه .

– bleeding.

tanzuf damm

تنزف دم .

Entertainment

General

Is there ... anywhere?

hal yoojad ... fee 'ay makaan?

هل يوجد . . . في أى مكان ؟

–a discotheque

marqaS (stayriyu club)

مرقص (ستيريو كلوب)

–a night-club

naady layly

نادى ليلى

–a jazz-club

naady djaaz

نادى جاز

–a casino

kasseenu

كازينو

–a zoo

Hadeeqat Hayawaan

حديقه حيوان

–a playground

mal9ab

ملعب

–a circus

seerk

سيرك

–a fair

madeenat malaahy

مدينه ملاهى

Where is it?

'ayn hiya

أين هى ؟

Where can I buy tickets?

'ayn yumkin shiraa' tadhaakir

أين يمكن شراء تذاكر؟

Cinema/Theatre

Have you any tickets for tonight?

9indakum tadhaakir lihaadhih 'allaylah

عندكم تذاكر لهذه الليلة ؟

Can I book a ticket for tomorrow?

mumkin 'aHjiz tadhkarah lilghadd

ممكن أحجز تذكرة للغد ؟

What's on....

maadhaa yu9raD

ماذا يعرض . . . .

–tomorrow?

ghadan

غدا ؟

on Sunday?	**yawm 'al'aHad** يوم الأحد ؟
–next week?	**'al'usboo9 'alqaadim** الأسبوع القادم ؟
Is it	**hal hoowa** هل هو . . . .
–good?	**jayyid** جيد ؟
–funny?	**muDHik** مضحك ؟
–exciting?	**mutheer** مثير ؟
–a musical?	**mooseeqy** موسيقي ؟
–a comedy?	**hazly** هزلي ؟
– a thriller?	**mughaamaraat booleesiyyah** مغامرات بوليسيه ؟
Two tickets, please	**tadhkaratayn min faDlak/faDlik** تذكرتين من فضلك .
At the back.	**fee 'alkhalf** في الخلف .

At the side.	9alaa 'aljaanib
	على الجانب .
At the front.	fee 'al'amaam
	في الأمام .
(Not) on the gangway.	(lays) 9alaa 'almamarr
	(ليس) على الممر .
In the	fee
	في ....
–stalls.	'almaqaa9id 'al'amaamiyyah
	المقاعد الأماميه .
–circle.	'albalkoon
	البلكون .
–gallery.	'albalkoon 'al'a9laa
	البلكون الأعلى .
–middle.	'alwaSaT
	الوسط .
–no-smoking section.	qism ghayr 'almudakhkhineen
	قسم غير المدخّنين .
What time does ... start?	fee 'ay waqt tabda'
	في أى وقت تبدأ ....
–the play.	'almasraHiyyah
	المسرحيه ؟
–the main film.	'alfilm 'alra'eesy
	الفيلم الرئيسي ؟

–the programme	**'albarnaamij**
	البرنامج ؟
Have you got any programmes?	**9indakum baraamij maTboo9ah**
	عندكم برامج مطبوعه ؟
May I have a programme, please?	**mumkin 'aakhudh barnaamij min faDlak/faDlik**
	ممكن آخذ برنامج من فضلك ؟
*I'm sorry, we've sold out.	**'aasif/'aasifah nafadhat kulluhaa**
	آسف نفذت كلها .

Of course, many of these questions and phrases can be used for other forms of entertainment and spectator sports.

NOTICES

No photographs	**mamnoo9 'attaSweer**
	ممنوع التصوير .
No children under 18 admitted	**mamnoo9 dukhool man hum doon thamaaniyat 9asharat sanah**
	ممنوع دخول من هم دون ثمانيه عشره سنه .

The Beach

Is it safe to swim here?

'assibaaHah 'amaan hunaa

السباحه أمان هنا ؟

Is it safe to dive here?

'alghaTs 'amaan hunaa

الغطس أمان هنا ؟

Is it safe for children?

fee 'amaan lil'aTfaal hunaa

في أمان للأطفال هنا ؟

Is there a life-guard?

fee munqidh

في منقذ ؟

*There's a strong current here.

fee tayyaar qawy hunaa

في تيار قوى هنا .

*It can be dangerous.	**mumkin yakoon khaTar** ممكن يكون خطر .
I'd like to hire....	**'ureed 'isti'jaar** أريد إستئجار ....
–a deck-chair.	**kursy lishshaaTi'** كرسي للشاطىء .
–a sunshade.	**shamsiyyah** شمسيّه .
–a cabin.	**kabeen** كابين .
–a boat.	**qaarib** قارب .
–a pedalo.	**pedalo** بيدالو .
–a surf-board.	**lawH rukoob 'al'amwaaj** لوح ركوب الأمواج .
–some water-skis.	**mizlaajaat maa'iyyah** مزلاجات مائيه .
I'd like to....	**'ureed 'an** أريد أن ....
–go fishing.	**'adhhab liSayd 'assamak** أذهب لصيد السمك .

–go underwater-fishing.	'adhhab liSayd 'assamak taHt 'almaa' أذهب لصيد السمك تحت الماء .
–go water-skiing.	'adhhab littazalluj 9alaa 'almaa' أذهب للتزلج على الماء .
–go surfing.	'adhhab lirukoob 'al'amwaaj أذهب لركوب الأمواج .
For one hour.	limuddat saa9ah لمدة ساعه .
For two hours.	lisaa9atayn لساعتين .
For the morning.	lifatrat 'aSSabaaH لفترة الصباح .
How much is it?	kam 'al'ujrah كم الأجره ؟
Per hour?	fee 'assaa9ah في الساعه ؟
Per day?	fee 'alyawm في اليوم ؟
Are there any showers?	hal yoojad doosh هل يوجد دوش ؟
Where can we buy a drink?	'ayn naqdir 'an nashtary mashroob أين نقدر أن نشتري مشروب ؟

Where can we get something to eat?	'ayn naHSal 9alaa shay' lil'akl

أين نحصل على شىء للأكل ؟

NOTICES

ممنوع السباحه

Bathing prohibited	mamnoo9 'assibaaHah

ممنوع الغطس

Diving prohibited	mamnoo9 'alghaTs

شاطىء خاص

Private Beach	shaaTi' khaaS

شاطىء عام

Public Beach	shaaTi' 9aam

للعائلات فقط

Families Only	lil9aa'ilaat faqaT

خطر

Danger	khaTar

Note: It is not safe to swim when a red flag is flying.

Sightseeing

Where's the nearest tourist office?	'ayn 'aqrab maktab siyaaHah أين أقرب مكتب سياحه ؟
What do you recommend me to visit?	maadhaa tanSaH/tanSaHy 'an 'azoor ماذا تنصح أن أزور ؟
Where is it?	'ayn أين ؟
Is there anything of interest here?	fee shay' shayyiq hunaa في شيء شيّق هنا ؟

Which is the most interesting....	'ay 'akthar tashweeq
	أى . . . أكثر تشويق
–museum?	matHaf
	متحف ؟
–church?	kaneesah
	كنيسه ؟
–mosque?	masjid
	مسجد ؟
–district?	minTaqah
	منطقه ؟
Where is....	'ayn
	أين . . . .
–the mosque?	'almasjid
	المسجد ؟
–the cathedral?	'alkaathidraa'iyyah
	الكاثدرائيه ؟
–the museum?	'almatHaf
	المتحف ؟
–the art museum?	matHaf 'alfunoon
	متحف الفنون ؟
–the castle?	'alqal9ah
	القلعه ؟

–the old part of town?	**'alqism 'alqadeem min 'almadeenah**
	القسم القديم من المدينه ؟
–the bazaar?	**'assooq**
	السوق ؟
–the Cedars?	**'al'arz**
	الأرز ؟
–the pyramids?	**'al'ahraam**
	الأهرام ؟
–the Sphinx?	**'aboo 'alhawl**
	أبو الهول ؟
–the monastery?	**'addayr**
	الدير ؟
–the University?	**'aljaami9ah**
	الجامعة ؟
–the amusement park?	**madeenat 'almalaahy**
	مدينة الملاهى ؟
–the zoo?	**Hadeeqat 'alHayawaan**
	حديقة الحيوان ؟
–the cave	**'almaghaarah**
	المغارة ؟
–the ruins?	**'al'aathaar**
	الآثار ؟

–the racecourse?	**maydaan sibaaq 'alkhayl** ميدان سباق الخيل ؟
–the tower?	**'alburj** البرج ؟
Is there a coach tour of the town?	**hal hunaak jawlah munaZZamah bilbaaS Hawl 'almadeenah** هل هناك جوله منظّمه بالباص حول المدينه ؟
Can one take a boat trip on the river?	**mumkin 'alqiyaam biriHlah nahriyyah fee qaarib** ممكن القيام برحله نهريّه في قارب ؟
Where does it leave from?	**min 'ayn tabda' 'arriHlah** من أين تبدأ الرحله ؟
How much does it cost?	**kam tukallif** كم تكلّف ؟
What time does it leave?	**fee 'ay waqt tabda' 'arriHlah** في أى وقت تبدأ الرحله ؟
What time does it get back?	**fee 'ay waqt yarji9 'alqaarib** في أى وقت يرجع القارب ؟

Is there an open market?	**fee sooq makshoof fee 'assaaHah**
	في سوق مكشوف في السّاحه ؟
Is there a market every day?	**fee sooq kul yawm**
	في سوق كل يوم ؟
Is there a guide?	**fee daleel**
	في دليل ؟
Have you got a guide-book?	**9indakum kitaab daleel**
	عندكم كتاب دليل ؟
In English, please	**bil'ingleezy min faDlak/faDlik**
	بالإنجليزى من فضلك .
Is there a reduction for students?	**fee khaSm liTTullaab**
	في خصم للطلاب ؟
–children?	**lil'aTfaal**
	للأطفال ؟

NOTICES

ممنوع التصوير .

No photographs to be taken	**mamnoo9 'attaSweer**

Other Leisure Activities

Where's the nearest ...	'ayn 'aqrab
	أين أقرب . . .
–golf club?	naady golf
	نادى غولف ؟
–swimming pool?	birkat sibaaHah
	بركة سباحه ؟
–ice-rink?	Halaqat jaleed lil'inzilaaq
	حلقة جليد للإنزلاق ؟
–tennis court?	mal9ab kurat maDrib
	ملعب كرة مضرب ؟
–football stadium?	staad kurat qadam
	ستاد كرة قدم ؟

–sailing club?

naady shiraa9y

نادي شراعي ؟

Does one have to be
a member?

laazim yakoon 'alwaaHad
9uDoo

لازم يكون الواحد عضو ؟

How much does it cost
to join?

kam yukallif 'al'ishtiraak

كم يكلف الإشتراك ؟

I'd like to hire.

'ureed 'isti'jaar

أريد استئجار

I'd like to take lessons.

'ureed duroos

أريد دروس

I'm a beginner.

'anaa mubtadi'

أنا مبتدئ

Can I fish here?

mumkin 'aSTaad samak hunaa

ممكن أصطاد سمك هنا ؟

Where can one fish?

'ayn yumkin Sayd 'assamak

أين ممكن صيد السمك ؟

Must I get a permit?

laazim 'aakhudh rukhSah

لازم آخذ رخصه ؟

Is it an outdoor pool?

hal birkat 'assibaaHah
khaarijiyyah

هل بركة السباحه خارجيه ؟

Is it an indoor pool?

hal birkat 'assibaaHah
daakhiliyyah

هل بركة السباحه داخليه ؟

Is it heated?

hal hiya mudaffa'ah

هل هي مدفّاه ؟

Loss or Theft

Someone has stolen my ...	**saraq shakhS** سرق شخص . . .
I've lost my ...	**Dayya9t** ضيّعت . . .
–passport.	**jawaaz safary** جواز سفرى .
–driving licence.	**rukhSat 'alqiyaadah khaaSSaty** رخصه القياده خاصّتي .
–insurance certificate.	**shahaadat 'atta'meen khaaSSaty** شهادة التأمين خاصّتي .
–car keys.	**mafaateeH sayyaaraty** مفاتيح سيارتي .

−log book.	**daftar yawmiyyaaty (mudhakkaraaty)** دفتر يومياتي (مذكراتي) .
−money.	**fuloosy** فلوسي .
−traveller's cheques.	**shikkaaty 'assiyaaHiyyah** شيكاتي السياحيّه .
−credit cards.	**biTaaqaat kradit khaaSaty** بطاقات كراديت خاصّتي .
−plane ticket.	**tadhkarat 'aTTaa'irah khaaSaty** تذكرة الطائره خاصّتي .
*When/Where did you lose it?	**mataa/'ayn 'aDa9tahaa** متى / أين أضعتها ؟
My ... has disappeared.	**... 'ikhtafat** إختفت . . .
−camera	**'aalat 'attaSweer khaaSaty** آلة التصوير خاصّتي .
−wallet	**miHfaZaty** محفظتي .
−jewellery	**mujawharaaty** مجوهراتي .
−handbag	**jizdaany** جزداني .

−briefcase

Haqeebat' alyadd khaaSSaty

حقيبة اليد خاصّتي .

*When did you last have it?

mataa kaanat ma9ak 'aakhir marrah

متى كانت معك آخرمره ؟

It was in my....

kaanat fee

كانت في . . . .

−car.

sayyaaraty

سيّارتي .

−room.

ghurfaty

غرفتي .

−beach-cabin.

kabeen 'ashshaaTi'

كابين الشاطىء .

Numbers

$\frac{1}{4}$	rub9	2	'ithnayn
١/٤	ربع	٢	إثنين
$\frac{1}{2}$	niSf	3	thalaathah
١/٢	نصف	٣	ثلاثة
$\frac{1}{3}$	thulth	4	'arba9ah
١/٣	ثلث	٤	أربعة
0	Sifr	5	khamsah
٠	صفر	٥	خمسة
1	waaHid	6	sittah
١	واحد	٦	ستة

7	sab9ah	19	tis9at 9ashar
٧	سبعة	١٩	تسعة عشر
8	thamaaniyah	20	9ishreen
٨	ثمانية	٢٠	عشرين
9	tis9ah	21	waaHid wa 9ishreen
٩	تسعة	٢١	واحد وعشرين
10	9asharah	22	'ithnayn wa 9ishreen
١٠	عشرة	٢٢	إثنين وعشرين
11	'aHad 9ashar	30	thalaatheen
١١	أحد عشر	٣٠	ثلاثين
12	'ithnaa 9ashar	40	'arba9een
١٢	إثنا عشر	٤٠	أربعين
13	thalaathat 9ashar	50	khamseen
١٣	ثلاثة عشر	٥٠	خمسين
14	'arba9at 9ashar	60	sitteen
١٤	أربعة عشر	٦٠	ستين
15	khamsat 9ashar	70	sab9een
١٥	خمسة عشر	٧٠	سبعين
16	sittat 9ashar	80	thamaaneen
١٦	ستة عشر	٨٠	ثمانين
17	sab9at 9ashar	90	tis9een
١٧	سبعة عشر	٩٠	تسعين
18	thamaaniyat 9ashar	100	mi'ah
١٨	ثمانية عشر	١٠٠	مائة

200	mi'atayn	800	thamaanmi'ah
٢٠٠	مائتين	٨٠٠	ثمانمائة
300	thalathmi'ah	900	tis9mi'ah
٣٠٠	ثلاثمائة	٩٠٠	تسعمائة
400	'arba9mi'ah	1,000	'alf
٤٠٠	أربعمائة	١٠٠٠	ألف
500	khamsmi'ah	2,000	'alfayn
٥٠٠	خمسمائة	٢٠٠٠	ألفين
600	sitmi'ah	1,000,000	milyoon
٦٠٠	ستمائة	١٠٠٠٠٠٠	مليون
700	sab9mi'ah		
٧٠٠	سبعمائة		

Combinations of numbers are formed thus:

131	mi'ah wa waaHid wa thalaatheen
١٣١	مائة وواحد وثلاثين
372	thalaathmi'ah wa 'ithnayn wa sab9een
٣٧٢	ثلاثمائة واثنين وسبعين
1,250	'alf wa mi'atayn wa khamseen
١٢٥٠	ألف ومائتين وخمسين

Numerical expressions

three-quarters	thalaathat 'arbaa9	ثلاثة أرباع
two thirds	thulthayn	ثلثين
a lot	katheer	كثير

a little	qaleel	قليل
a few	biD9	بضع
more	'akthar	أكثر
less	'aqall	أقل
double	Di9f	ضعف
half	niSf	نصف
once	marrah	مرّة
twice	marratayn	مرّتين
three times	thalaath marraat	ثلاث مرّات
millions of	malaayeen min	ملايين من . . .
countless	laa yu9add	لا يعدّ

Cardinal numbers

first	'awwal	أوّل
second	thaany	ثاني
third	thaalith	ثالث
fourth	raabi9	رابع
fifth	khaamis	خامس
sixth	saadis	سادس
seventh	saabi9	سابع
eight	thaamin	ثامن

| ninth | taasi9 | تاسع |
| tenth | 9aashir | عاشر |

The Time

| Excuse me. | tismaHly/tismaHeely |
| | تسمحلى . |

What's the time, please?

kam 'assaa9ah min faDlak/faDlik

كم الساعه من فضلك ؟

It's one o'clock (exactly).

'assaa9ah waaHidah (tamaaman)/(biDDabT)

الساعة واحدة
(تماما) / (بالضبط)

It's (nearly) two o'clock.

'assaa9ah (taqreeban) 'ithnayn

الساعه (تقريبا) إثنين .

It's just after three o'clock.

'assaa9ah ba9d 'aththalaathah biqaleel

الساعه بعد الثلاثة بقليل .

It's ... past three.

'assaa9ah thalaathah wa

الساعه ثلاثة و . . . .

–a quarter

rub9

ربع .

–half

niSf

نصف

–ten minutes	**9ashr daqaa'iq**
	عشر دقائق .
It's ... to four	**'assaa9ah 'arba9ah 'illaa**
	الساعه أربعة إلاً . . . .
–a quarter	**rub9**
	ربع .
–twenty minutes	**9ishreen daqeeqah/thulth**
	عشرين دقيقة / ثلث .
At two o'clock	**9ind 'assaa9ah 'ithnayn**
	عند الساعه إثنين .
It's midday.	**'al'aan 'aZZuhr**
	الآن الظهر .
It's midnight.	**'al'aan niSf 'allayl**
	الآن نصف الليل .

Some Time Phrases

At night.	**fee 'allayl**
	في الليل
In the morning.	**fee 'aSSabaah**
	في الصباح
–afternoon.	**ba9d 'aZZuhr**
	بعد الظهر
–evening.	**'almasaa'**
	المساء

At midday.	9ind 'aZZuhr
	عند الظهر
At midnight.	9ind niSf 'allayl
	عند نصف الليل
Today.	'alyawm
	اليوم
Tommorow.	ghadan
	غدا
Tonight.	'allaylah
	الليله
Last week.	'al'usboo9 'almaaDy
	الأسبوع الماضي
–month.	'ashshahr
	الشهر . . . .
–year.	'assanah
	السنه . . . .
Next week	'al'usboo9 'alqaddim
	الأسبوع القادم
–month.	'ashshahr
	الشهر . . .
The day after tomorrow.	ba9d ghadd
	بعد غد
Yesterday.	'albaariHah
	البارحه

The day before yesterday.	**'awwal 'albaariHah**
	أول البارحه
This morning.	**hadhaa 'aSSabaaH**
	هذا الصباح
This afternoon.	**ba9d Zuhr 'alyawm**
	بعد ظهر اليوم
This evening.	**hadhaa 'almasaa'**
	هذا المساء
I'm sorry I'm late.	**'assif/'assifah ta'akhkhart**
	آسف تأخرت
I'm afraid I'm early.	**'akhshaa 'anny mubakkir/mubakkirah**
	أخشي أني مبكر
See you later.	**'araak/'araaky ba9dayn**
	أراك بعدين
See you tomorrow.	**'araak/'araaky ghadan**
	أراك غدا
Now.	**'al'aan**
	الآن
Soon.	**qareeban**
	. قريبا
As soon as possible.	**fee 'aqrab waqt mumkin**
	. في أقرب وقت ممكن

One day.	**yawman maa**
	يوما ما .
The other day.	**dhaalik 'alyawm**
	ذلك اليوم .
In a minute.	**fee daqeeqah**
	في دقيقه .
In a few minutes.	**fee biD9 daqaa'iq**
	في بضع دقائق .
Earlier.	**fee waqt saabiq**
	في وقت سابق .
Later.	**ba9dayn**
	بعدين .
In a week's time.	**khilaal 'usboo9**
	خلال أسبوع .
In a month's time.	**khilaal muddat shahr**
	خلال مدة شهر .
Wait a minute.	**'intaZir/'intaZiry daqeeqah**
	إنتظر دقيقه .

The months are the Gregorian names pronounced in dialect Arabic. A European would have no difficulty and there is no need to list them. (**yanaayir** for January, **septambar** for September etc.)

On the other hand, a visitor to Saudi Arabia may come across the Hijri months and it may be useful to list them. The more common thing in the Gulf, though is to name a month by its serial number (January is referred to as month one, May as month five etc.)

HIJRI CALENDAR MONTHS

muHarram	محرّم
Safar	صفر
rabee9 'al'awwal	ربيع الأول
rabee9 'aththaany	ربيع الثّاني
jamaadaa 'al'awwal	جمادى الأول
jamaadaa 'aththaany	جمادى الثّاني
rajab	رجب
sha9baan	شعبان
ramaDaan	رمضان
shawwaal	شوّال
dhoo 'alqi9dah	ذو القعده
dho 'alHijjah	ذو الحجّه

Days of the week

Monday	'al'ithnayn	الإثنين
Tuesday	'aththulaathaa'	الثلاثاء
Wednesday	'al'arbi9aa'	الأربعاء
Thursday	'alkhamees	الخميس
Friday	'aljum9ah	الجمعه
Saturday	'assabt	السبت
Sunday	'al'aHad	الأحد

on Monday	**fee yawm 'al'ithnayn**
	في يوم الإثنين
every Saturday	**kul sabt**
	كل سبت
last Tuesday	**'aththulaathaa' 'almaaDy**
	الثلاثاء الماضي
next Friday	**yawm 'aljum9ah 'alqaadim**
	يوم الجمعه القادم
a week next Friday	**ba9d 'usboo9 min yawm 'aljum9ah 'alqaadim**
	بعد أسبوع من يوم الجمعه القادم
a week last Sunday	**ba9d 'usboo9 min yawm 'al'aHad 'almaaDy**
	بعد أسبوع من يوم الأحد الماضي
except Sundays	**maa 9adaa 'ayyaam 'al'aaHaad**
	ما عدا أيّام الآحاد
every other day	**yawm ba9d yawm**
	يوم بعد يوم
a fortnight	**'usboo9ayn**
	أسبوعين
a month	**shahr**
	شهر
a year	**sanah**
	سنه

The Seasons

spring	'arrabee9	الربيع
summer	'aSSayf	الصيف
autumn.	'alkhareef	الخريف
winter.	'ashshitaa'	الشتاء

in spring.   fee 'arrabee9

في الربيع

during the winter.   khilaal 'ashshitaa'

خلال الشتاء

in summer.   fee 'aSSayf

في الصيف

a summer dress.   fustaan Sayfy

فستان صيفي

a winter holiday.   9uTlah shatawiyyah

عطله شتويّه

Winter sports.   riyaaDah shatawiyyah

رياضه شتويّه

a summer cold.   rashH Sayfy

رشح صيفي

The Months (serial numbers – see p. 157)

January	'kaanoon 'aththaany	كانون الثّاني
February	shubaaT	شباط

March	'aadhaar	آذار
April	neesaan	نيسان
May	'ayyar	أيّار
June	Huzayraan	حزيران
July	tammooz	تمّوز
August	'aab	آب
September	'aylool	أيلول
October	tishreen 'al'awwal	تشرين الأوّل
November	tishreen 'aththaany	تشرين الثّاني
December	kanoon 'al'awwal	كانون الأوّل

in May	fee ayyaar
	في أيّار
next March	'aadhaar 'alqaadim
	آذار القادم
last June	Huzayraan 'almaaDy
	حزيران الماضي
at the beginning of April	fee 'awwal neesaan
	في أوّل نيسان
at the end of July	fee 'aakhir tammooz
	في آخر تموز

Colours

beige	bayj	بيج
black	'aswad	أسود
blue	'azraq	أزرق
brown	bunny	بنّى
cream	'aSfar baahit	أصفر باهت
	(bilawn 'alqishTah)	(بلون القشطة)
crimson	'aHmar qirmizy	أحمر قرمزى
gold	dhahaby	ذهبي
grey	ramaady	رمادي
green	'akhDar	أخضر
orange	burtuqaaly	برتقالي
pink	zahryy	زهري
purple	banafsajy	بنفسجي
scarlet	'aHmar faaqi9	أحمر فاقع
silver	fiDDy	فضي
white	'abyaD	أبيض
yellow	'aSfar	أصفر
dark (brown)	(bunny) ghaamiq	(بنّي) غامق
light (blue)	('azraq) faatiH	(أزرق) فاتح
bright (red)	('aHmar) faaqi9	(أحمر) فاقع

Countries

I come from	'anaa min	. . . . أنا من
Australia	'ustraaliyaa	أستراليا
Austria	'annamsaa	النمسه
Brazil	'albaraazeel	البرازيل
Canada	kanadaa	كندا
England	'inglitarrah	إنجلترا
France	faransaa	فرنسا
Germany	'almaanyaa	ألمانيا
Greece	'alyoonaan	اليونان
Holland	hoolandaa	هولندا
India	'alhind	الهند
Ireland	'irlandaa	إيرلندا
Italy	'eeTaalyaa	إيطاليا
Japan	'alyaabaan	اليابان
Mexico	'almakseek	المكسيك
New Zealand	niyoo zeelandah	نيو زيلانده
Pakistan	'albaakistaan	الباكستان
Peru	'alpirroo	البيرو
Portugal	'alburtughaal	البرتغال
Scotland	'iskutlandah	إسكتلنده

South Africa	janoob 'ifreeqiyaa	جنوب افريقيا
Spain	'aspaaniyaa	أسبانيا
The USA	'alwilaayat 'almuttaHidah 'al'amirikiyyah	الولايات المتحده الاميركيه
Wales	waylz	وايلز

Nationalities

(In modifying feminine nouns, add (ah) and remember that the words marked + + are invariable)

I'm	'anaa	. . . . أنا
an Arab	9araby	عربي
Australian	'ustraaly	أسترالي
Austrian	namsaawy	نمساوي
Brazilian	baraazeely	برازيلي
Canadian	kanady	كندي
French	fransaawy	فرنساوي
German	'almaany	ألماني
Greek	yoonaany	يوناني
English	'ingleezy	إنجليزي
Dutch	hoolandy	هولندي
Indian	hindy	هندي
Irish	'irlandy	إبرلندي

Israel	'israa'eely	إسرائيلي
Italian	'eeTaaly	إيطالي
Japanese	yaabaany	ياباني
Mexican	makseeky	مكسيكي
A New Zealander	niyoo zeelandy	نيو زيلاندي
Pakistani	baakistaany	باكستاني
Peruvian	min pirroo	من بيرو
Portuguese	burtughaaly	برتغالي
Scottish	'iskutlandy	إسكتلندي
South African	min janoob 'ifreeqiyaa	من جنوب افريقيا
Spanish	'aspaany	أسباني
North American	min 'amirikaa 'ashshamaaliyyah ('amreeky)	من أميركا الشمالية (أميركي)
Welsh	min waylz	من وايلز

ARABIC

J. R. SMART

A clearly structured introductory course designed to help you achieve basic fluency in modern international Arabic.

The Arabic taught in this book is the written and spoken language used as the *lingua franca* of the Arab world. Designed as a self-teaching course rather than as an Arabic grammar in the traditional sense, the book begins with a detailed introduction to the Arabic script and pronunciation. Each of the first ten units then deals with a specific aspect of Arabic grammar and sentence construction, which is clearly and simply explained and practised in a variety of exercises. Units 11–18 contain illustrative texts dealing with various aspects of Arab life, with new grammatical points being picked out in analyses and special sections. The book concludes with appendices dealing with the complexities of the Arabic verb and Arabic numerals, a key to the exercises and a concise Arabic–English vocabulary.

TEACH YOURSELF BOOKS

Quick & Easy

The Quick and Easy series of short courses is designed to enable the reader to get by at a survival level. Offering more than a phrasebook, each course focuses on the key language likely to be needed on a visit abroad. The travel packs, which each include a book and an accompanying cassette, make indispensable travelling companions.

Languages available in the series are:

Arabic	Japanese
French	Portuguese
German	Russian
Greek	Spanish
Italian	Turkish

A selection of further titles
from Hodder & Stoughton / Teach Yourself

0 340 27582 0	Arabic – book	£6.99	☐
0 340 41950 4	Arabic – book/cassette pack	£15.99	☐
0 340 51959 2	Chinese – book	£8.99	☐
0 340 58513 7	Chinese – book/cassette pack	£17.99	☐
0 340 49231 7	Turkish – book	£6.99	☐
0 340 49551 0	Turkish – book/cassette pack	£15.99	☐

All Hodder & Stoughton / Teach Yourself books are available from your local bookshop or can be ordered direct from the publisher. Just tick the titles you want and fill in the form below. Prices and availability subject to change without notice.

To: Hodder & Stoughton Ltd, Cash Sales Department, Bookpoint, 39 Milton Park, Abingdon, OXON, OX14 4TD, UK. If you have a credit card you may order by telephone – 01235 831700.

Please enclose a cheque or postal order made payable to Bookpoint Ltd to the value of the cover price and allow the following for postage and packing:

UK & BFPO: £1.00 for the first book, 50p for the second book and 30p for each additional book ordered up to a maximum charge of £3.00.
OVERSEAS & EIRE : £2.00 for the first book, £1.00 for the second book and 50p for each additional book.

Name...

Address ....

....

....

If you would prefer to pay by credit card, please complete:
Please debit my Visa / Access / Diner's Card / American Express (delete as appropriate)
card no:

Signature...Expiry Date ....